Sister Nations

NATIVE 🐦 VOICES

Native peoples telling their stories, writing their history

Sister

Nations

*Native American Women
Writers on Community*

Foreword by Winona LaDuke

Edited by Heid E. Erdrich & Laura Tohe

 MINNESOTA HISTORICAL SOCIETY PRESS

Native Voices

Native people telling their
stories, writing their history

To embody the principles set forth by the
series, all Native Voices books are embla-
zoned with a bird glyph adapted from
the Jeffers Petroglyph site in southern
Minnesota. The rock art there represents
one of the first recorded voices of Native
Americans in the Upper Midwest. This
symbol stands as a reminder of the enduring
presence of Native Voices on the American
landscape.

Publication of Natives Voices
is supported in part by a grant
from The St. Paul Companies.

www.mnhs.org/mhspress

Manufactured in the
United States of America

10 9 8 7 6 5 4 3 2 1

♾ The paper used in this publication
meets the minimum requirements
of the American National Standard
for Information Sciences—Permanence
for Printed Library materials, ANSI
Z39.48-1984.

International Standard Book Number
ISBN 0-87351-427-0 (cloth)
ISBN 0-87351-428-9 (paper)

Library of Congress
Cataloging-in-Publication Data

Sister nations : Native American women
writers on community / edited by
Heid E. Erdrich and Laura Tohe
    p. cm.
Includes bibliographical references.
ISBN 0-87351-427-0 (cloth : alk. paper)
ISBN 0-87351-428-9 (pbk. : alk. paper)
  1. American literature—
     Indian authors.
  2. Indians of North America—
     Literary collections.
  3. Women—United States—
     Literary collections.
  4. American literature—
     women authors.
  5. Indian women—Literary collections.
  6. Community—Literary collections.
  7. Indians of North America.
  8. Women—United States.
  9. Indian Women.
 10. Community.
  I. Erdrich, Heid. E. (Heid Ellen)
 II. Tohe, Laura.

PS508.I5 S57 2002
810.8′09287′0997—dc21

                    2001057986

Contents

3 ¤ New Age Pocahontas 107

4 ∗ *In the Arms of the Skies* 151

Foreword

Ikwewag diibaajimowag. Ikwewag nagamowag. Bizindan, Bizindan. Agindaasonnan, agindaasonnan.

The women are telling stories, the women are singing, listen, listen. Read, read.

Remarkable memories spill forth through pens held in the hands of dishwashers, hands of baby carriers, hands of loved ones and lovers, and the hands of those who hold the almighty bingo dauber.

In this book, you will find cherished memories and intimate stories revealed as the treasures they are. Some with the simplicity and matter-of-factness of a conversation or a tied quilt. Others with the intricacy and detail of the quill work on a hide using the smallest of quills from the porcupine's side.

Storytelling is an artform, and the span of stories shared here is a mosaic. They are breathtaking, from the cherished oral histories of Changing Woman, recording the path, "the miikinaa," the Creator has offered to women, to the honest memories of grandmas and quilts.

My eyes see these pages and remember these women, when we were all young. I have had the privilege of knowing many of them, either as fine friends and acquaintances, or as women I have simply admired through the years. *She is walking on the prairie at Standing Rock, long hair loosely braided. She and I listen intently to the words of others, a wonder at it all. Her smile is radiant, her hands record the words, and her heart remembers.* I remember another of these women, remarkable at a young age as well. I remember her determined, deep within research documents of our people, like an onion, peeling back the layer after layer of stories. *Her brow is furrowed, her smile shy, yet weary with the memories of ancient names, the heartache of old ones. I remember her*

and am amazed at her tenacity and earnestness. I am a bit daunted.
For another woman, I remember her laughter. It is like a beautiful waterfall, the same as her hair, cascading around her angular face, but her laughter and lilting voice stays in my head for the months that will pass until I see her again.

Then there are the many stories of the women I only know through their writing, I await, patiently, when possible, each new offering, each new gift. For their stories are those I am hungry for, the stories kept secretly, cached away for generations, never to see a publisher. For their stories are from far away mesas, huge trees, and raging rivers I visit only in my mind. For their stories are often my own, and in the telling of them I am reminded of my own humanity. I am reminded of the joy and sorrow that fills our lives. I am reminded of a phrase, carved into a wall in Guatemala: "Altogether we have more death than they, but altogether we have more life than they." And I know it is true, especially when I miss those who have already gone ahead to the spirit world, women who walked these same paths as those in this book.

And so it is, I, like many of these women here, find I am compelled to live, to read, and to write. To tell these stories, and honor each other, our tales of life, and our memories when we pass on. It is twenty years since I remember many of their faces, and I look at us now, I see our bodies transformed to the softness of bellies that have borne children, to the hands that have fashioned clay, butchered deer, and washed many dishes. And I am blessed with their writing, words, and memories, because they are amazing.

Winona LaDuke
December 2001

Introduction

Writing the introduction to this anthology is like a naming ceremony. All the relatives have come together to celebrate this new thing that is just now going out into the world to make her voice—voices—known. We pause to wish her well on her way and to pray for her journey. The name has been dreamed and now we speak it: *Sister Nations*, as we remember how it came to be and thank all who came before it.

This anthology got its start when my friend, poet and editor Jim Cihlar, suggested I edit a collection of Native American women's writing. As we talked about the project, Jim wondered what point of coherence such an anthology might find and I immediately suggested a theme of community. I had thought about such a collection of writing for some time. Whenever anyone mentions the oral tradition and storytelling, I think of the stories Native American women tell among themselves. Not the traditional tales, although there are those, but the jokes, love life woes, gossip, and memories we all share. The greatest gift of being born into the Indian* world might be the friend-ship, the kinship, that comes from talking with Native women from many nations. If women writers from the hundreds of tribes and indigenous communities in North America had felt that blessing as well, then I knew we could have our book. So we began to gather voices that would explore the warmth, the fierceness, the cutting humor, and the tough love that is the heart of "Indian Country," that is the Native American woman in her world, in our world.

Of course there have been other collections of Native Women's writing, and it is only right to say, humbly, that Rayna

---

* See notes for discussion of interchangeable use of Indian, Native American, Indi'n, and other terms.

Green's *That's What She Said* and Joy Harjo and Gloria Bird's *Reinventing the Enemy's Language* are ancestors to whom *Sister Nations* owes debt. Still, the scarcity of books that have collected Native American women's writing—what amounts to one major publication a decade for the past three—makes clear the need for an anthology that not only shows the variety and complexity of Native women's roles in society, but that holds those writings closely together in a particular and relevant context.

We sent out a call that asked for poems and prose that "celebrated, recorded, and explored aspects and traditions of Native American women's communities." We wanted work that would be of interest to both an audience familiar with such traditions and to one being introduced to the lives and ways of contemporary Native American women. Our hope was that Native American readers and students might recognize their own experience in some of the selections, and non-Native Americans might learn something about their neighbors and friends.

I'm grateful that Jim Cihlar suggested I ask Laura Tohe, who had been his colleague at the University of Nebraska, to be my co-editor. Laura is Navajo, a published poet, and professor of American Indian Studies at Arizona State University in Tempe. She brought an interest and knowledge of the Southwest tribes to complement my own interest in tribes of the northern Great Lakes and Plains areas. Together we began the long process of reading manuscripts by over a hundred writers who responded to our open call and by others whom we solicited ourselves.

The experience of reading the words of so many Native American women and girls was humbling, moving, and a great honor. We made selections based on the theme of community as well as on the quality of the work we received. There were a great deal many more poems and stories we would have liked to have had the chance to publish, and we hope that we will be able to read those words in another book someday.

Otoe-Missouria/Muscogee writer Annette Arkeketa sent us a manuscript of student writing that would make a powerful book on its own. One poem, "About Me," written by then seven-year-old Whitney Hernandez, somehow reveals the spirit we saw in all the submissions:

In the Kickapoo village
We have friends and family.
Sandra, Amanda, Armando, Frank,
Ramon, Freddie Jr., Jose, Jose Jr.,
Irene my mom.

Sometimes my grandpa and me
play together
like hide and seek.

Ready or not here I come.

We received work from writers who represented more than twenty tribes and communities in a dozen states from the U.S., and from Canada and Mexico. We read poems and stories by great-grandmothers, social workers, farmers, and professors. We learned about fishing in Alaska and burning cedar in Oklahoma. In the end, Laura and I also became aware that many of the submissions we received were from women of our own respective tribal groups. In some ways it was not surprising to find we had attracted submissions from writers in our own areas—we are both active in supporting writing by our tribal sisters, and our tribes are two of the largest indigenous populations in the U.S. We might have called this *Sisters North and South* and made it a Navajo-Ojibwe anthology; we read that much excellent work from both groups. But we wanted to show how the sense of kinship, so important to indigenous communities, crosses boundaries of culture, even political boundaries imposed on land. In our final selections we were aware of voices from each of the four directions, from beyond the borders of the U.S., and from a variety of ages and stages in life and in writing. We are pleased to have work by such established authors as Joy Harjo and Roberta Hill along with work by emerging writers Teresa Iyall-Santos and Linda Noel and others.

The fact that my two sisters Lise Erdrich and Louise Erdrich contributed stories makes me proud and humble; we have only once before been published together, and the work you will see from them here speaks deeply of family and sisterhood in just the way I had hoped for the anthology. It is also a great honor to publish my tribeswomen, Anishinaabekweg: kateri akiwenzie-damm, Kimberly Blaeser, Pauline Danforth, Linda LeGarde Grover, Sara Littlecrow-Russell, and Marcie Rendon.

In arranging the anthology by theme, Laura and I discussed common concerns of the work we had chosen. We placed the work into four sections: "Changing Women," "Strong Hearts," "New Age Pocahontas," and "In the Arms of the Skies."

The first section, "Changing Women," reveals the power of transformation in the female experience. Poems and prose for that section deal with the stages of a woman's life, girlhood, maturation, adult life and/or pregnancy, and becoming an elder. These writings also reveal an awareness of our female ancestors, and women's traditions of healing and making art. The second section we titled "Strong Hearts" and, as it suggests, the poems and prose here show Indian women enduring with love: defending with fierce judgment, reaching out across history to protect the people. Section three, "New Age Pocahontas," reveals the humor and complexity of our reactions to the stereotypes and simplified images of Native American women. The final section, "In the Arms of the Skies," contains poems of love and sex along with prose works, such as Joy Harjo's "In the Arms of the Skies," that put typical notions about romantic love to the test. As we read these sexy, sweet, and sly poems and stories, I couldn't help but think of the Ojibwe stories about Star Husbands and stories common to many tribes in which the beloved takes the woman to live in the sky. This section makes clear that women from many Native nations think of love or sex in terms of the landscape as the final poem in the anthology, "the way around losing you" by Kimberly Wensaut, reveals: "my heart is only a metaphor for the way the earth holds her secrets."

Each of the four sections is introduced in a brief essay by the editors. Rather than review the whole book here in the introduction, we chose to provide comment that introduces the work as you read, and that focuses on the themes and questions we see contained in each section. Also contained in the anthology are notes on the text, information on tribes, and a brief biography of each author often accompanied by comments on her work and a list for further reading.

I began my introduction with an analogy to a naming ceremony—but I left out the important fact that at the end of most ceremonies, at least up north, there is a feast. The food is always good and there's only one rule: eat it all! Reader, I invite you to this feast in the hope you will feel, as I have always felt in the company of Native American women, an ease like coming home, along with a keen awareness of our life in this land, of our abiding relation to our sister nations.

Heid E. Erdrich
St. Paul, Minnesota
November 2001

>>

In January 2001 Heid and I met in Chinle, Arizona, to organize the manuscript in terms of subthemes. I, too, was impressed and honored to have the work of writers emerging and established in my care. As we read for theme, we discussed the invisibility of Native women in comparison to men, and we remarked that Native women are often represented by popular culture within the Plains Indian context, the generic Indian. Omnipresent is the "squaw" who is portrayed as servant, concubine, beast of burden, drudge, "sinful," and "sultry." Her image continues to deny Native women their distinct identities. Such dreadful images are often found on covers of romance novels while the name is given to mountains, resorts, and at least one highway.

In Chinle we talked of the need for an anthology that would reveal more complex pictures of Native Americans. Today any tourist shop in the Southwest abounds with postcards of romantic images of women and girls dressed in turquoise and pictured against a picturesque background such as Monument Valley, a flock of sheep, a weaving loom, red rocks, and so forth. The Indian maiden, placed on cigar boxes, maps, postcards, greeting cards, ads generate marketable value. She is princess, comforter, and gives aid; she is Pocahontas who saves a white man; she is the female Noble Savage, Sacajawea, who helps white men. In the movies her character dies having done her part to aid white men. The "Cherokee Princess" possesses Asian or white features to make palatable to western tastes, thus the Barbie doll look found in tourist shops, magazines, toy stores, and grocery shelves. Her image sells.

In the New Age movement, the Native woman becomes the symbol of spiritualism. She is connected to and is one with nature. She talks to animals and is imaged with an owl, coyote, or a wolf. She possesses ancient knowledge and communicates with higher powers using crystals and amulets. She represents what western culture has lost and is trying to regain.

Such images of Native women, framed as they are in terms of colonial hetero-patriarchal values, needs, guilt, and made for commercial use, creates a construct of the colonizer that invents and distorts the images of Indian women. The represented voices in *Sister Nations* break through the crusty layers of stereotypes. Here are Native women from many nations who define themselves and their communities on their terms. Like Changing Woman, who embodies the transformative power of women, these Indian women are telling their lives with humor, honesty and within the context of becoming.

Laura Tohe
November 2001

Acknowledgments

For assistance in editing this anthology, we must acknowledge our debt to the Loft Inroads program and the Native Arts Circle Writers founding members: Jon Bell, Pauline Brunette Danforth, Roberta Hill, Franklin Firesteel Lenor Scheffler, and Kim Wensaut. Without you we would not have known how to collect *Sister Nations*. Thanks to past New Rivers Press staff who got this project off the ground: James Cihlar, Phyllis Jendro and the late C.W. (Bill) Truesdale, a longtime publisher of Native American writing. Thanks as well to final Minneapolis staff of New Rivers, Lisa Bullard and Eric Braun, who placed the basket on the Minnesota Historical Society Press doorstep for adoption. Several interns and students helped with the many tasks of keeping this book in order: Kelly, Sunny, Bethany, and Kira, thank you.

To the Minnesota Historical Society Press editorial staff, Ann, Greg, and Ted: we are grateful beyond words for your leap of faith in picking up the manuscript, for your patience in dealing with the details of a multiple-author collection, and especially for the respect you extended to us in welcoming us to the Native Voices series.

To Deborah Miller of the Minnesota Historical Society, a great thanks for the award of a research grant, part of which supported work that took place during final editing of *Sister Nations*.

We further wish to thank the editors of the following magazines and publishers, where some of these pieces originally appeared, often in earlier forms: *The New Yorker* for Louise Erdrich's "The Shawl," *Cimarron Review* for LeAnne Howe's "Choctalking on Other Realities," *Gatherings* for Suzanne Rancourt's "Sipping," *Futures* for Marcie Rendon's "what's an indian woman to do?" and the University of Arizona Press for Karenne Wood's poems, which appeared in earlier versions in *Markings on Earth;* and Esther Belin's poem "From the Belly of My Beauty," which appeared in *From the Belly of My Beauty.*

»

My patient husband John Burke gave up much to help in my work and for that my heart-thanks and ultimate respect. Jules Ezra, thanks for being such a good boy while Mama worked! My most humble thanks to my assistant/literary midwife Martha Furman who took this project through its difficult final stage of labor. Martha, could not have delivered without you. Miigwech.

Heid E. Erdrich

»

Thanks to my mother Laura Florence, whose stories flow through me, to Cheryl Clayton, and to my female and male friends who inspire me with their own stories of the power of the human spirit.

Laura Tohe

Sister Nations

1 Changing Women

In the oral tradition of the Diné they say a baby girl was discovered atop one of the sacred mountains in Dinétah in the Fourth World. This baby was raised and cared for by First Woman and First Man. Changing Woman, also known as White Shell Woman, was a special child who came to the world to save it. She is a holy person like White Buffalo Calf Woman and Christ. When she became a young woman, she went through the first Kinaalda, a puberty ceremony. This transformative event marks a time of ceremony and celebration in which the family, clan, and community are involved. There is no shame, mystery, or fear of the natural processes of maturation and aging. With age comes life experience, knowledge, and wisdom for which there is respect. During the ceremony the initiate embodies the spirit of Changing Woman. To the Diné she is Asdzàà Naadlee'hí, who birthed the Twin Heroes who made the world safe for habitation. By taking parts of her body, Changing Woman created the four principal clans. Changing Woman transforms herself according to the seasons of the year from childhood and through each of life's stages until she reaches old age. When spring arrives she transforms into a beautiful young woman again, hence her name.

While the Changing Woman is part of the Navajo Blessing Way, she also represents the life stages of all women whose lives are continually in the process of transformation and re-creation as daughter, sister, mother, aunt, and grandmother. The works included in this section acknowledge Native women's experience and wisdom connected to indigenous knowledge despite disruption, oppression, and banishment by colonialism and patriarchy. The voices speak of women's roles and responsibilities in the continuance of family and nation, women united in the duties of burial rituals and renewal and, above all, kinship ties to earth and community to create a stable and growing society, for it is often the women who form the backbone of their nations.

Here are voices from traditional oral literatures and from women raised in cities who still identify with their ancestry "back home." Here are voices that speak of the worship of youth and the invisibility of old age ubiquitous in popular culture.

The written art collected here leaves a legacy of how Native women are bound through blood, history, through the healing power of humor and language. The voices expressed here reveal the transformative and re-creative abilities of being female, of being changing women. And using the common language we call English, we continue to tell our stories and our lives, for to have no stories is to be an empty person.

Laura Tohe

kateri akiwenzie-damm » Anishinaabe

Sleepwalker
(for VW)

eyes close like bones cracking
a raven eating stones at a curve of road
grinding in the gullet
rotting flesh spit between split lips
each day a slow act of dying
calling underworld creatures to ankles clicking
the path more luminous
begins in the navel
stretches
twists
tangles

(grandfather
do you see me approaching?)

there is a storm front moving inside my head
the air is heavy
the leaves still
waiting
for the storm to break
us open

the haze will rise
disappear
like spirits in the night sky

i eat wild leeks
milkweed greens
old photographs
faces without names

my own
stranger
moon pulls blood from me
pale i shiver
store feathers in my cheeks
my songs have broken wings
invocations hit the ground
like hatchlings

(grandmother
lead me where the medicine grows)

fossil backbone
branches snapping
no splints no casts no healing
just neckbones drying in my throat
a floor of crushed vertebrae
mats woven of cartilage and veins

i rub bear grease ointment
on my belly
paint my face with clay

pull the day over my shoulders
like a shawl

bury myself
hugging shadow babies to my breasts
the smell of milk sweet
on their breath
fills my lungs
with forgetting

chant carved bone in elm bark basket
dried salmon floating with half eaten hearts
desiccated ovaries swimming in blood

i
fall
asleep
in a house of old bones

dream

sapphire fiddleheads
glowing
under my fingers

and later
ribbons of pink in a raging winter sky

Esther Belin » Navajo

First Woman

Emerged from the everlasting clay at the bottom
of Cañon Diablo

Now she walks down Cerrillos toward the plaza
the clay still part of her
bundled in velveteen inside her knapsack
ready for the first display window with the right price

She walks on
wanting to hail a ride
yet wanting her limbs to mark the pavement
ever so lightly with blood and flesh and
    quarter-century-plus-old bones
and usually Coyote picks up her scent and comes
    sniffin' around

Yá'át'ééh' abíní
Aoo', yá'át'ééh', First Woman says
wishing she just walked on
but he knew her tongue
paused to look with both eyes
wide open
bright like sunny-side-up eggs
With big teeth and smile Coyote asks, háágóóshą'?
Plaza'góó and before he can respond First Woman adds,
Shí k'ad dooleeł, hágoónee'
First Woman turns halfway to get the side ways view
dark hair catching the sun skews her image
and sure enough Coyote
still there
chuckles and says, hazhó'ígo, hazhó'ígo . . .

First Woman breathes
focusing the fire within her
tending her own heat
back then
the fire was her first child
Her body
a wood-burning stove
giving her cravings for chili
hot and spicy, rich with flavor and settling with heat
later taking it back with nightmares or itchy breasts or
    sore tailbones
Her womb
a cauldron
boiling or simmering
her temperature still a little offset
and First Woman
breathes in the morning
and exhales the scent of wily Coyote
and First Woman
breathes in the white
light rays of the new morning
and coffee still hot enough to sip
and tailpipe exhaust
as she crosses the railroad tracks ever closer toward the plaza

Kimberly Blaeser » Anishinaabe

Shadow Sisters

We could meet them bent over the bait bucket, or feet glued
to the pedals of a sewing machine. We could watch them, legs
crossed desperately, hobbling off laughing in the direction of
the woods or the outhouse. Or find them walking midnight
floors with an infant who mews its feverish approach to truth.

Cooking food they couldn't afford, smoking away a new coat,
never weighing the price of love. Dark hair, dark eyes, dark skin,
bruised lives they neither earned nor much took notice of.
Children guarded, their treasured coins of hope.

Sixty-four years they trade kindnesses, gossip, jealousies. We
watch them play saint and sinner, switching roles at silent cues.
They are sisters. As different as one snowflake is from the other;
as much the same. Somewhere in that space between likeness
and dissimilarity, eternity burns. Somewhere a feuding protec-
tive devotion. Two sisters, unmindful of the mark of history.
Laugh carelessly, daughters. Rock wildly upon the lap of story.

1951. Together they drove an abandoned boyfriend's pickup
truck 270 miles on the back roads between St. Paul and Nay-
tah-waush. Because neither could steer, clutch, and change gears
simultaneously, they traveled locked together in a bizarre version
of a three-legged race, one steering and braking, one clutching
and shifting. Dripping with the sweat of fear, they cursed and
cried their way into a new syncretism, were baptized into a
laughing grace that ever after revisited them in times of crisis.

1953. 1955. 1959. Birth years. *When you play you pay,* they
joked, swaddling the fussy longings of youth, wrapping them
tightly with the responsibilities of babies, Minnesota heating
bills, and beer battles.

1965. Toes sink into cold tilled reservation earth. Seeds sift
through fingers. They are women planting dreams with dank
names like rutabaga and kohlrabi. Extending their own black
turnip feet under the icy hose all summer. Stocking the hollow
fall root cellar. Filling canning jars with the colors of summer,
the scents of winter suppers: purple pickled beets, golden corn,
eel-shaped slippery jims, green beans, dill pickles, sauerkraut.
Arranging them on shelves late at night; gifts upon an altar.

1967. One construction worker, one daddy, one volatile lover
crushed by a North Dakota night train, buried deeper than
memory. Three-legged, the families limp on.

1970. Giddy games of canasta played too late into autumn nights
when everything is on the verge of falling. Decks of kittens and
mountain scenery mixed madly together, wild cards and red
threes coveted like someone else's husband. Children and parents learning math, adding game points and allegiances.

1973. Wounded Knee Indians scowl into cameras on every
channel. Five-time election judges, these sisters know tribal
politics never change. Indian dreams for justice stillborn these
many generations. But there is a restlessness that settles now
beneath their chests, fluttering like the first movement of small
life within a woman's body.

1977. Driving together again, thermos of coffee and cigarettes
between them, they make five A.M. departures for electronics
assembly line jobs seventy-five miles away. Return for late night
bartending. Everything just another road trip leading back home.
To picnics and birch bark Sundays, croquet and crappie fishing.
To children who come and go in their own frenzied migrations,
anchored by that same whispered weight of longing.

1980. At the horseshoe bar, old flames surface behind the moist amber of a beer glass. Everyone acts like they are still in love. In a hard week, sleep comes more easily if they pretend they believe it. Sometimes in the cold of January, they forget they are pretending.

1982. 1985. In the polyester years they become grandmothers. Sisters dizzy with the time-lapse passage of their lives, they brush wisps of hair from wrinkled foreheads, from still nut-dark eyes, as if they could dispel the bewilderment of rebels falling into grace. At last, courting the danger of acknowledgment, over fish entrails or quilt pieces they puff out small questions, see them rise and expand like smoke rings. Gray circles hover between them, truant halos never asking *How much?* or *How many?* But *Why do you suppose? How come?* And *What we gonna do?*

1988. Losses multiply as first a knee joint goes, then the good ear. The last parent, one brother, two nephews, three women friends from way back when. When the roll of reservation dice takes its toll, old hearts still break.

1992. Shooting Star. Northern Lights. Firefly Creek. They visit all the casinos. Indians everywhere are coming out, celebrating five hundred years of survival. These women have been out their whole lives, know survival like a long hangover. Tastes like castor oil sometimes or like bitten-down tears, but it's been getting easier to swallow every year. Sweet like maple sap when you see a child off to a new-growth tribal college.

Legacy is not a word these sisters use. Their English doesn't bend to it. Still they wear the strands of history like strings of colored trade beads. Memorial days they visit all the old graves. Keep the names from rusting on the tongue. Teach their children to welcome the repetition of stories.

Like that they notice other reservation sisters. Mismatched and inseparable. Watch when one half falls away. The other left out of step, lost, unable to recognize her lone shadow. Two sisters sharing the comfort of community gossip, they mourn each separation, silently fold away fears of their own. Each plans to live longer, to spare the other the grief and loneliness.

Years bend around this pact. They wake in the new millennium, not certain if they are still surviving or just the ghost spaces that waver in time, markers shimmering with the significance of past lives. Thought we saw them just the other day sitting together outside the new clinic, one still smoking to keep the piety of age at bay. *Joined at the hip.* That's what my sister says.

Elizabeth Cook-Lynn ≫ Dakota

A Woman's Old Age

She had come to the time of her life
when she had to struggle
to defend her innocence;
cynicism came much too easily
like handsome birds of prey moving in
stealthily, disgorging tufts of bone,
eliminating frightened and watchful
rodents

In this silence
in this cave of bound things
she and the man she has lived with
off and on for fifty years
have never learned the darkness of
each other's souls because
everything has stood for
high and mighty values

It is only from the casual things
that you can walk away

Pauline Danforth » Ojibway

Piece Quilt: An Autobiography

Quilts and afghans in a rainbow of colors are the legacy left to me by the strong women in my family. These blankets remind me of the love and connectedness I feel with my mother, grandmothers, and aunts. When I wrap myself in these quilts, their spirits surround me, protecting me and giving me strength.

My quilts and afghans are stored in a large brown trunk with rusty hinges that I inherited from my Ojibway grandmother, Nancy Kettle or Pe-wa-bick-oquay meaning Iron Woman. She was given this trunk back in the 1930s depression by a neighbor who had recently immigrated to northern Minnesota from Finland. My mother talked about the trading and sharing that occurred among the Finns and Indians on the Ponsford prairie. My mother would carry eggs to the new neighbors and would return with a pail of fresh cow's milk. The Finns and Indians on the Ponsford prairie relied on one another in those lean years.

My relatives accepted new ways, and in turn, were generous with their immigrant neighbors. Through all the generations, we as Indian people have both shared with and adapted to the white world, retaining some of the old ways and adapting to new circumstances. My blankets remind me that my relatives were a sharing people.

My trunk holds my star and wedding ring quilts, both made by the Ojibway women at the Catholic church guild hall. My star quilt in faded shapes of turquoise, red, and purple and my wedding ring quilt in beige and peach tones are my oldest and most treasured blankets. When I touch them, I see my grandmother Nancy quilting with the other women, all bent in a large circle around their latest quilt. In my vision, the late afternoon sun streams through the tall, west-facing windows. In soft musical tones, the women are talking in Ojibway, laughing and gossiping in their shared task. Several children, including myself, come in from the government day school down the road a short distance. We forget to shut the door and a grandmother chides us, "Gigin waa naa giziwis," meaning, you've got a long tail. Most of us born in the 1950s understand Ojibway, though few of us can answer in our native tongue. We play tag, scrambling over chairs and under tables until we are told to sit still.

Until I was eight years old I lived with my grandmother in Ponsford, a small community perched on the edge of Minnesota's prairie land. My mother worked an erratic nurse's aide shift in Minneapolis and felt I had better care with my grandmother. Traditional Ojibway families took care of one another, often informally adopting children or old people without families. Grandma was "Mom" to me and other grandchildren, as well as to four orphaned nieces and nephews whom she raised.

When I was a young child in her care, she was strong, chopping us wood to fuel our barrel stove. She was also stubborn and independent, refusing to have electricity and indoor plumbing installed in our four-room tarpaper house. We hauled our water from the red pump outside the house and on Sunday nights, my cousin Mary Anne and I would bathe in a square metal tub next to the kitchen stove. On school nights, I did my homework by kerosene lamplight and listened to the crackling, battery-powered radio.

Mom was spiritual, somehow incorporating both Catholic and Ojibway Midewiwin beliefs. From the bedroom at night I would hear her talk to the gi-bye or spirits that visited her as she sat up doing jigsaw puzzles in the kitchen. She explained that sometimes she perfumed, like from a wake. In deference to both her beliefs, she sprinkled holy water and burned sage to send the restless spirit on its way, saying, "Go on ma-jan, ma-jan."

The wedding ring quilt is made of cotton pieces salvaged from Mom's everyday work dresses. The gingham and calico pieces can be seen in old family snapshots. This quilt reminds me of my role as a woman. I am an only child, but I grew up surrounded by cousins and extended family members. I didn't really think of having a family until my mother died in 1985. She left a hole in my heart that friends just couldn't fill.

Twelve years after she left on her spiritual journey, my son came to me in a typical Ojibway fashion. Nathaniel, who was born in 1997, is the grandson of my cousin Mary and great-grandson of my Auntie Ione. Nathaniel's mother was unable to care for him; he needed a home and Mary wanted him to stay within the family and so he joined my branch of the family tree. My blankets and the stories they tell will someday belong to him.

The wedding ring quilt with its many connecting circles, so much like our lives, was patched by Auntie Ione. The backing had worn thin and so she sewed a durable green polyester backing onto it. Auntie Ione was like that, always patching up us kids' skinned knees and trying to catch us to wash our dirty faces. My cousins and I would hide under one of the rusty iron beds in my grandmother's house. Auntie would get a broom and poke at us, teasing us that Ben Skip will have us for dinner if we didn't come out. Ben Skip-in-the-day was a neighbor on the reservation with an undeserved reputation for eating naughty little children. Even today, the myth of Ben Skip keeps little children in line.

Auntie Ione was a special aunt. When I lived with Mom, she lived across the road with her husband and seven children. She had a big family of her own, but she always had love enough for me. When I was lonely for my mother, so far away in Minneapolis, Auntie Ione hugged me. In traditional Ojibway culture, aunts are special—they are second mothers. Auntie Ione was my other mother.

In the decades since World War II, Indian people have moved to the cities in ever increasing numbers until today more Indians live in cities than on reservations. My family was part of the migration of Indian people moving to cities for jobs and opportunities.

I was eight years old when I moved to Minneapolis to live with my mother. Soon after, Grandma Mom had her first stroke and joined us in a four-room basement apartment. Mom still did her jigsaw puzzles, but now her tormenters were flesh— the social workers who haunted us for details of our lives. She would angrily pull the shades when they knocked on our door. When my mother allowed them in, she scolded them in Ojibway, telling them to mind their own business and leave ours alone.

The city had other obstacles for Mom. One evening as we were rushing to catch a bus to St. Paul to visit Auntie Ione's family, Mom hobbled along getting all out of breath. Now a coltish ten-year-old, I scampered ahead and begged the bus driver to wait for Mom. He wouldn't and I was so hurt. The rush of the city was just too much for her. She lived with us two years before she had a second stroke and moved to a nursing home. She lost some memory and speech and was frustrated by her inability to communicate with us. My mother, her main caretaker, bore the brunt of her frustrations. Yet she never complained, saying she was grateful to have her mother with her still.

After six years in a nursing home near our apartment, Mom moved to a nursing home in a town near the reservation. A week before she was to visit the community where she had spent her life, she fell from her wheelchair. Mom went home the next week, but in a box.

By this time I was in college at Bemidji State University. My mother taught me to value education. After she had hurt her back working as a nurse's aide, she became a housemaid, cleaning the homes of professors along East River Road. She wanted a life like theirs for me, not the hard life of a maid. She told me, "Babe, you finish school so you won't have scrubmaid knees like me." Often I went along to these homes to help. I discovered an exciting world in their studies, lined with books and photographs of their travels. My mother made me believe that I could have a better life with an education.

Very few of my aunts, uncles, or cousins have finished high school, much less gone on to college. When I first left home for college, my great-aunt Jenny Ellis, or Grandma Jenny as we called her, made me a quilt in pink and blue hues. The 1970s psychedelic print fabrics were left over from my own sewing attempts. The quilt was a gift toward my college education. College was a milestone and Grandma Jenny acknowledged it with her gift.

My step-grandmother Isabelle Brunette, or Grandma Nette, sewed the heavy green and yellow corduroy quilt for me. My stepfather drank a lot and was mean to my mother. Yet the quilt is not about their troubled marriage but is about the special relationship I had with Grandma Nette, a very old woman of French-Canadian and Ojibway descent.

We had a unique camaraderie. She would call me from her little home on the White Earth Reservation and chuckle, "When are you taking this old bag of bones driving again?" She weighed less than one hundred pounds. Her thin frame was topped by a halo of white hair secured with rhinestone combs. Sometimes when I drove over from Cass Lake where I was living, we would drive to her family burial plot on a hillside cemetery overlooking the western plain of Minnesota. On these drives, she would regale me with tales of her youth in Calloway where she grew up in a large family of sisters. She described being the belle of the ball at the local dances. She spoke lovingly of the older, handsome man she married, then outlived by fifty years, never again marrying.

One bright sunny day, we drank 3.2 beer at a country honky-tonk. Grandma Nette's daughter Frances and her deaf sister Pude were along. We played the jukebox and shuffled around the dance floor teasing Grandma Nette about her younger dancing days, saying, "When you were young, I bet no one could keep up with you." We had a great time dancing in the middle of the day with just a slight 3.2 beer buzz. As afternoon turned into evening and the sun set over Toad Lake, I wondered if

Grandma Nette would ever get tired and want to go home. She lived six more years, dying at age ninety-six.

Finally and most importantly, my trunk shelters the many afghans made for me by my mother, Elizabeth Kettle Brunette. She made afghans only for those most dear to her. Since I have five, she must have loved me a lot. For many years I doubted that love because I felt she had abandoned me with my grandmother. It took years for me to see what a gift she gave me, allowing me to live with Grandma Mom. She gave afghans to a few select friends of mine; three were given to girlfriends whose friendships she shared and two were given to boyfriends she hoped I would marry. One of whom I did, much later.

Besides the afghans, her other enduring gift to me was her respect for and curiosity about our Ojibway cultural roots. Through lots of storytelling, she gave me her memories of growing up on the Ponsford prairie. She was a skilled story-teller, weaving me wonderful stories of her childhood, all the while teaching me Ojibway values including respecting the land and honoring one's family.

Through hours of listening to her, I came to know intimately the land allotted to her grandmother, Wah-we-yay-cumig-oquay or Round Earth Woman. She described the cabin in which she lived and the hill where she played. I can see her as a girl sitting next to the Ojibway gravehouse of her deceased aunt, Jane Kettle. Her grandparents told her to go there and keep her aunt company. They told her, "Your aunt's spirit lingers there and must be respected. Go, eat with your aunt." So along with her sisters, brother, and cousins, she carried a spirit dish to her aunt and a picnic lunch for themselves.

She shared stories about her childhood conflict between the Catholic and the Midewiwin religions practiced by her different sets of grandparents. Grandpa Kettle would chide her, saying, "You go into that church and throw your hind end up in the air. What does that accomplish?" He tried scaring her, telling her that she wouldn't be allowed in the white heaven nor the Indian heaven, but would be like a rabbit sitting outside chewing on twigs. My mother said the more Grandpa Kettle scolded her, the more fervently she attended Catholic mass.

Together one spring day before she became terribly ill, my mother and I visited Grandpa and Grandma Kettle's homestead site which was then a farmer's field. We searched for remnants of buildings she remembered. We discovered the old root cellar. She pointed out where the log cabins and barn once stood. Finally, we visited the small cemetery where her aunt, father, and other relatives are buried beneath small gravehouses in the Midewiwin fashion. Weathered by rain, wind, and falling branches from the basswood trees and disturbed by grazing cattle for many years, only fragments of the gravehouses could be found. We quietly placed tobacco where they once stood.

Mother was pleased when my interest in Ojibway history led me to a land claims research job in the Cass Lake Bureau of Indian Affairs archives. I gained access to old correspondence and land records detailing how the White Earth Ojibway, including my family, lost their allotted lands. I researched our genealogy, tracing our family back to Flatmouth, an important mediator between white people and Ojibway Indians in the 1860s. My mother marveled at the information I unearthed. I found the Ojibway names of aunts, names she had forgotten. I found a letter composed in 1910 by her grandfather, Mike Kettle or Ne-zhe-gwon-e-ge-shig. He spoke with passion about the land-hungry, thieving people trying to rob him of his daughter's land allotment. He spoke of hunger and of a traditional world in chaos.

A generation later and three hundred miles away, my mother had different changes to cope with. Like many other Indians, she left the reservation during World War II to work for the war effort. She never returned except to visit. Her world was the dirty inner-city neighborhood where she could afford to live. She practiced some of the old ways of her grandparents. Before a storm, she would find the cleanest place in the littered backyard of her apartment building to leave tobacco, asking the Thunder Beings to spare her family from their fury.

She gave me the last afghan she crocheted. She called it her scrap afghan because it was made of leftover yarn. Maybe she knew her life was almost over and wanted to weave together these remaining skeins. She finished it just before her final battle with the cancer she had fought valiantly for eighteen years.

Soon after she left her apartment for good, going to a palliative center, a fancy name for a place people go to die. Her only wish was a bed with a view of the sky. I wanted to believe she would get better and I talked of the times we would walk to the park across the street. She sent me back home to Cass Lake twice, saying she was feeling much better. She really didn't want me to see her pain which was constant in the end. She refused pain pills, telling me they blurred her visits with her sisters, cousins and friends.

My last visit, I bargained, "Now you make it to my birthday. I want you there at my party." But she was giving up on future plans here. Instead she talked of long-dead aunts and grandmas who came to visit, telling her it was okay to come home to them. In that sterile room my mother gave me her final gift. For years, she tried remembering the Indian name given to me by an old woman from our community. As she lay dying, my mother remembered that name. She said it was Ke-we-tah-be-nais-equay, meaning "bird that flies lightly from tree to tree."

Like that bird, I am constantly exploring the two worlds I live in. I've lived in both reservation and urban communities. I value the past and the stories of my relatives' survival. They taught me change could not be stopped. Yet, the cycle of life continues. People die, but new life is born from the old. Traditions falter, but as long as the spark remains in us, our ways will continue and we as Ojibway women will endure.

Susan Deer Cloud » Mohawk/Blackfeet

Welcome to the Land of Ma'am

Welcome to The Land of Ma'am, where countless Indians
perished because brazen, young invaders erected
their "Land of the Free" on Turtle Island, Mother Earth.
Welcome to The Land of Ma'am, where you are free
to be young, smooth-skinned, strong—
    free to call women with silver
gracing their long hair *Ma'am*. Welcome, you who
    stand indifferent
as the godlike models in *Vanity Fair,* you GAP boys with bulges
of retro-testosterone in your khaki pants, addressing
    women like me
in John Wayne drawls, *Excuse me, Ma'am,* if you see us at all.
    Welcome
to moon-drawn decades of walking on Earth,
    to wise-woman hair,
to faces carved with petroglyph-wrinkles, myths in flesh.

And welcome, you who are young and female,
    blonde and glittering
with rings in noses, ears, tongues—you who are pricked
with bold tattoos on the drunken dough of derrières bouncing
like swing music beneath the jive of high skirts.
    To you, especially, welcome
to The Land of Ma'am, girls serving me in restaurants, stores—
confident your waists will never expand, nor black
    witch hairs sprout
on your chins overnight, nor the charmed cells of your
    tinseltown behinds
migrate like disoriented geese to your anorexic arms.
    Can I help you, Ma'am?
The nasal riptide of a sneer undercuts your deodorized *Ma'ams*.

Oh, doomed Lolitas of America's malls, Ophelias of the Big Mac
born with the silver spoons of Hollywood lies up your
     fixed noses, playing
bad girls, cracking into mad girls when you can't pretend
     you're perfect
products anymore—welcome to that land you're destined for.

Welcome to The Land of Ma'am, where the old grow invisible
inside "The Land of the Free." Welcome to the reservation
that the young, the powerful, the rich try to consign you to,
     as if you were
a cast-off dress with no body in it, fit only for a thrift shop,
     mothballed
purview of the poor. And welcome to the end of sex, where
     "Wham, bam,
thank you, Ma'am" shrivels into new meaning—no bodies
     over twenty
allowed in this America of TV-programmed Crest-white teeth,
Jane-Fonda-implant breasts, contact-lens-throwaway-blue eyes,
collagen smiles, sucked-thin thighs. Who would want to
make love to decades of daydreams, longing, sorrow, ecstasy,
delicate wisdom glowing like wildflowers in moonlight—want to
kiss flesh like hills warmed by many suns, gullied
by stinging rains, hypnotic snows? Welcome to the land
of mammograms.

I say Ma'ams of the World unite, start your own goddess-business!
I say make "Ban the Ma'am" buttons, then wear them proudly
on red tee-shirts, your breasts soft and low and braless
     underneath!
Every chance you get, thrust out buttons of defiance
on street corners, at malls, universities, movie houses,
     banks, the halls

of Congress, yes! Ma'ams, snatch back this land and
    don't plead *"pretty*
pleeease!" Dream it the way it was before the tribes
    were divided, crushed,
when older women were revered as beautiful elders,
    medicine women,
wise women, beloved women, when the People cried
for their visions in the female heart
of the ancient hills.

Ma'ams, it's a good day to die.

Nicole Ducheneaux » Sioux/Flathead

Picking Indian Tea

In her jeep, through the bowing canopy of ponderosa pines,
we lurch,
we three.
She wears her hair in that bottle-black French twist,
    though she is tall and has felled any number of elk
    in long melted winter snow.
And even though those hands are crooked at the joint now,
swirling lopsidedly in husky gesticulation,
she'll be there again when we are home for the fall
and the Mission Mountains sigh with their spreading
    whiteness.
So we ride, I in the makeshift back seat, swinging my
    Velcro sneaker feet,
and she tells the story of the chewed-up rosary and
    old Resurrection Sam, who rose from the dead once
    in the Mission church to the sound of sobbing laughter.
"Oh, yes. Old Resurrection Sam, I remember him,"
    my mother says.
And honeyed flashes of leafy light spray down on us as we ride,
we three,
up the north fork of the Jocko.
And, yes, there's a story about him too.
Who knows how far up into the sky we have rattled yet
in my clumsy dream of walking through the gray blanket
    of a cloud,
but the sun is shining today.
So with the low shrubs on either side we stoop,
we three,
touch the tender leaves and pluck them like precious emeralds
    from the stalk.
"These are best for Indian tea," holding up a silky one, says she.

And when we've filled our shopping bags up to their
    hiccupping tops,
we follow her into the trees to search for huskusk root—
a delicate task.
The plant, hung with veiny tattered lace,
hides in the arms of a deadly twin—the philosopher's end
    and the bitter cure.
"You gotta' be careful what you pick."
And she pulls it up out of the earth,
the thirsty hairs dripping soil like sweat.
We take it home, over the road, into the valley.
I rest in the afternoon, in the coffee air,
just me,
reading seven tattered generations of *Redbook* and *McCall's*,
and washing my hands for a thick stew dinner.
I never drink the tea.
It sits in a musty bag still, next to some yellow casserole dishes.
But I chew the root when I'm learning how to divide and
    multiply in a wide ruled book.
I swallow and sniff my thoughts into a mountain fog
    I've never known.
And the root is gone now,
though its scents the house in Tenelytown.

I wear your gloves,
holding my own red hand,
stitched with your name, Lucille.

Heid E. Erdrich » Ojibwe

Craving: First Month

My belly rejected everything but a certain sky,
the one that rocks the high north plains of home.
The streaks of cirrus like pale sweet lettuce:
to tear a leaf and taste that clear covering of clouds!
Nothing but color and light for my mouth.
I craved the prairie, wild as Rapunzel's mother—
and would have paid the witch's price,
but my dear sister knew this dire appetite and agreed
to drive into the horizon, north and north for hours,
the car skimming along the two-lane blacktop
between acres of flooded field. We were asea
in the land that bred us. It fed us and we were happy.
The rush of passing color like fuel. Waves of chartreuse
mustard weed lapping the ditches, confusing waves of sky
grown on earth—flax blue as mirage, then a doe,
then her fawn springing blazingly, redly,
ahead of us against the new crown of hard wheat.

That's what I grew my son on, month one.
I went hungry into the flat north toward the reservation.
I ate it all. Even the dusty green of the little-leaf sage
that covers my grandparents' grave
tasted good in my eyes.
Here it is, I said into wind up the bald hill.
Here it is, I said to the question mark of child.
Here's the land we are born from; here's what made us,
here's the world that fed us, here now, you eat too.

» » »

She Dances

The drum begins and she
raises her hand to lift
the female-feathered fan.
She moves slowly, heavy
in her buckskin, heavy
with the possibility of life.
Her neat fringe beats along
with the drum as she steps.
Full sun in full leather and
she wills herself not to sweat.
I pray the long days in the arena,
nights sleeping on the ground,
make her ready to dance labor.

Though it's my right, I never dance.
Not in a shawl, with fluid moving fringes,
not with beads offered up leggings,
no satin-worked ribbons or cones sewn
in V-shapes have ever drawn an arrow down
my hips to point the way to being woman.

But I once dreamed my friend a dress:
one in slipping honey colors of satin
with black bands. Its music came with,
its cones jangling and flashing near each
flower-print cloth outfit then on to the next.
And now I dream her another dress,
the one for labor, a traditional: deep blue,
the midnight wool blue shot with red
that all her ancestors would recognize,
the heavy dress of history,
the one made of flags
and ration blankets and blood.

Allison Adelle Hedge Coke » Huron/Cherokee

In the Fields

1975. Sixteen. My birthday half a season away. In a few weeks I
would be settled. The families had agreed. The two of us worked
together side-by-side in these fields, and migrated for work as
well, in search of crops to pick—beans, potatoes, tobacco,
lemons—whatever was ripe and ready for harvest. We'd settled
together, back in North Carolina, where our southeastern Indian
ancestors had always been—home.

His mother was Indian, his dad a white man. We were both
mixed-bloods and bore the pain of taking urban jobs when the
fields went dry though neither of us could stand living in town
long, so we'd often end up sleeping outside, waiting for pay-
checks. For the last year we'd mostly lived in the car, hunting
in winter, fishing in summer, and following work in the fields.
An old man always came to wake us before the others got to the
field. A thin man with a face creased from smiles and weathered from working in the sun.

The sun rose as we moved from one plant bed to another.
Again and again, the men raised Visqueen, exposing green leaf
on black soil and we worked throughout the morning gathering
tobacco plants strong enough to survive transplanting to the
fields and replanting them. In this way we gave in to the rhythm
of fieldwork. The steady bend and rise, the motion of tending
new growth, opening and closing spaces in earth, creating patterns—motion, united in movement, much like communal
dance during celebratory and ceremonial times. There was a
glory in this motion. It often caused one to sing out loud and
sometimes the singing was so great the mighty sun felt as if it
gave way to the beauty of the sound and burned a little easier
down upon us in the rows.

The oldest woman was a grandma many times over. I'd
taken her some snuff and asked for help in learning to quilt.
She was next to me now, telling stories about these fields from

decades ago. Her arthritis made it impossible to work much, yet she came out every morning to help, mostly watching over the workers with smiles and sighs of approval. Looking at her hands, I remembered the top sheets my dad's mother left when she died. Unfinished quilts for her descendants pieced from a bag filled with scraps from homemade clothing remnants. My dad said fifty-pound bags of chicken feed and flour came in floral cloth bags when he was young, and two feed bags were enough cloth to make a dress; one would make a blouse or skirt. My dad was the youngest in the family and his mother would have him collect up the scraps for her at times. When he was around fourteen (1936), he drew a design for a quilt he called "Birds in the Garden."

The birds were made of triangles pieced together standing out against a blocked garden background. This is one of the quilts his mother never finished, though she did piece the top fully and pass it on to him. After working with this grandma on a few of her own quilts, and helping her clean cow guts, Birds in the Garden was the first one I finished myself. I didn't have a frame then. I'd used a large embroidery hoop to hold the cloth and batting tight. My dad came over and I showed him the work. I knew he was pleased because he took me out back and taught me how to construct a quilt frame which you could raise and lower from the ceiling with a rope-pull.

Here in the beds, I pulled another baby tobacco, the roots drawing dank scents, and remembered the smell of antique cotton from mysterious pieces of shirts, dresses, and skirts which came from ancestral clothing of strange designs, prints only familiar from seeing these quilt-tops in the wooden chest in my parents' room. Some of the quilt pieces older than my father came from my grandmother's family before her. The cloth travelled along with the family until this time. I presented the quilt to my younger brother so the passage would go female, male, female, male in the family. My grandmother collected the scraps. My father designed the pattern. My grandmother pieced the cloth. My father gave it to me. I quilted the batting and bottom sheet to the top and presented it to my brother, the youngest male of our generation.

"Birds in the Garden."

Just below where we worked, next to fields where we would transplant these seedlings, lay our own garden. I'd tilled the entire field weeks before, when the moon signaled planting. Every plant, each herb or food, was grown by its neighbor on the barter system. Each row was planted to assist opposing rows with their own growth. Beans produce nitrogen, corn plants need nitrogen, marigolds bordering the southern side repelled insects that eat up leaf, squash and pickling cucumbers ran the northern edge just below the tree line, mint kept the ants away, and so on.

After the plants passed a seedling stage, I kept no scare in the field to ward off birds and they helped pluck insects off the plants, bees hived an old tree not far away, and it seemed every bud must have pollinated because later that same summer the garden would outgrow any other for miles and miles. Even this early in the season, when fog and leaf, grey and green, swallowed the earth completely, I knew there'd be plenty. Each day grew hotter and hotter in the fields, the stretch of heat waving shoulder-high on the primer just ahead of you, and the same on the one behind. The heat-waves bringing rhythms and patterns of their own into those that came directly from priming leaves, you tucked them into elbow crooks until the space between your arms and body existed no more and you were carrying fifty pounds or more of fresh green tobacco, continuing for as long as the fields ran.

The pattern of motion from fieldwork stays with you: even in our sleep we primed, taking each leaf around the bottom for half a stalk, reaching in circular motions to grasp all four in a single round. We continued stuffing primed leaves under our arms until elbow crooks were pushed out ninety degrees and continued stuffing till they would hold no more. Each day, every minute in the field something green was appreciated and honored, and on the hottest afternoons I'd be brought by the field rhythms to certain praise, and pray for rain and sing to bring it on and my father-in-law would tell me to knock it off because he didn't appreciate us singing in Indian out in the fields. But when the rains came he was glad too, he just never said anything about it. We could all see it on his face and thought it peculiar he put up so much of a fuss when it was sure to come anyway. This was western North Carolina; rains were certain here.

Yesterday was stiff, sticky, weeding: bristled thistles or long slender unknowns which only a few generations ago were a known delicacy. Bees sampled blooms around me. I sang to them, low and soft, so they wouldn't fear me and grow angry. Each bee bringing her own story and song from the flowers to the comb. The hive sat not far from here in the wedge of a tree fork. The tree itself rough and hollow, refuge for the workers and their queen, a young grandma, a head dancer always organizing the hive simply by her motion and sacred scents, the honey a perfumed liquid quilt, and all around me a thousand scents: corn, peas, beans, cucumbers, melon vines, pumpkins, potatoes, mustard greens, collards, turnip greens and turnips, squashes of every shape and color, even bottle necks for drums and songs of their own, anise, mint, tansy, juniper, long-needle pine, cedar, scuppernong vines, thick rich earth black and raised, damp and fertile, and the weeds, those plants no longer relished in communities, yet perhaps more nourishing than all the rest combined. I thought, where did it go? Where was the natural gathering motion from long ago? The motion which consumed and compelled fieldworkers, bringing endurance to the labor in the sun. Motion which called us as Human Beings to sing, to dance, in the glory of all that is and will be. The rhythm of the world.

Here, it compelled me. I reached forward, grabbing a fresh shoot, looking for more, filling my pockets with tender green, saving roots to establish firmly in fresh ground. They were in my pockets still this morning and I knew I would find a place that they could grow. I relished the thought of weeds replanted intentionally and went on with my work.

Choctalking on Other Realities

There is only one pigeon left in Jerusalem. It could be the weather. Perhaps his more clever relatives took refuge in the cities by the Red Sea where the climate is better. Jerusalem occupies a high plateau in Israel/Palestine. In January 1992, record snows have fallen here. Outside our hotel, ice-covered oranges weigh the trees down like leaded Christmas ornaments.

I've come to Israel as an academic tourist on a university-sponsored tour. We're told that with few natural advantages and no indigenous raw materials, apart from stone, the economy of Jerusalem has always been supported from the outside. They're entirely dependent on peace. If that's true, we want to know why Jews, Muslims, and Christians in Jerusalem have adopted the stance of a "mobilized society." Perhaps it's their heritage. Each of these religious groups has always made great sacrifices to change the status quo. Recall the Jews taking Canaan and greater Israel; the Christians capturing the Roman Empire and the New World; and the Muslims seizing Arabia, Asia, and Africa. The wars of heaven.

I leave the National Palace Hotel in East Jerusalem and meander down a narrow street. The pigeon comes and goes. He sails above my head. I pass a park where the benches are vacant and gray. As the afternoon light creeps behind another ragged wall of snow clouds I stop. The bird lands just beyond my reach, and I throw him the remains of my falafel sandwich. A late breakfast. We eye each other until he draws his head back as if his attention is fixed in the distance on something no one else sees. Eventually I see it too. A group of women marches toward us chanting slogans in Arabic and the sky cracks open and the pigeon flies away.

They're Palestinians. Seven women. Their arms are linked together in solidarity like a chain of paper dolls. I don't understand what they are saying but I can guess. They want to change the status quo.

I follow the procession. After all, this is what I've come for. To see who is doing what to whom. Like peeping Toms or UN observers, we academics do very little except tell each other what we've seen. Always in dead earnest.

Soon tourists come out of the shops to see what all the ruckus is about. The women encourage us to join their protest. In a few minutes two blue and white trucks loaded with soldiers arrive carrying white clubs and tear gas launchers. The women stay together as long as they can until they are broken apart by the soldiers. Many of the tourists become frantic. They run into the soldiers or away from them. People scramble in all directions.

One woman breaks away from the others and runs in the direction of the American Colony Hotel. For some unexplainable reason I run after her.

Suddenly she's behind me. I know her by the sound of her feet running. I run faster across the dirt playground. If she catches me I'll never escape. I hear her panting loudly. Her weight and large frame knocks me down. I can't breathe. Her blonde face blushes red as she yanks me up by my arms.

I twist out of her grasp and run toward a fence made of chicken wire. Beyond it is the Wa-He Cafe in Bethany, Oklahoma. Indians are there drinking coffee and gossiping about the weather. If I make it to the Wa-He they'll protect me. But she tackles me again. Hammers my head with her elbow. Sweat pours out of her body and wets my face. I gag trying not to swallow. A second white teacher comes to her aid. Together they carry me toward a small building, the kindergarten school connected to their church. They open the broom closet and shove me inside. The door slams shut.

I am still running.

This Is the Story I Really Wanted to Tell

It was so hot in the kitchen of the Oklahoma City airport cafe that the plastic clock melted. Time oozed down the wall just like Salvador Dali imagined. The metal pieces of the flimsy clock went "clink, clank, ting" as they hit the floor. That's because the steaks were burning, the beans were boiling, and Nina the Ukrainian had pulled a butcher knife on Gretchen the German. There is a war going on. I am in uniform. But I race ahead of myself. This story begins in 1970.

First there are the characters.

Gretchen the German. A Catholic. The blonde cook with the white hairnet pulled down over her ears like a helmet. A Berliner, she escaped Nazi Germany during World War II to come to America and cook Wiener schnitzels. That's what she tells all the customers at the airport cafe.

Susan B. Anthony. The black, six-foot-tall night-cook-in-charge, Susan B. likes the blues. Speaks choicest Gullah. Cooks like snapping fingers in time. Her great-great-grandmother was a slave. Every night at the airport cafe she says, "Honey, don't mess with me." And I don't.

Nina. A Russian Jew from the Ukraine, she wears a white cotton uniform with socks held up by rubber bands. Nina's thumb is tattooed and causes people to stare impolitely. She says she escaped the massacre at Babi Yar. Each night she chisels perfect heads of lettuce into identical salads and weighs each portion. She is quite insane.

And me. An Oklahoma Choctaw. The waitress in the yellow uniform at the airport cafe. I'm a union steward for the International Brotherhood of Hotel, Motel, and Restaurant Workers of America; I'm nineteen years old and have been baptized many times. The Southern Baptists, the Nazarenes, even the Mormons got to me. Finally, I've given up being a religious consumer to become a socialist. The AFL-CIO is going to send me to college.

The Scene.
The airport cafe. Feeding time. The fall of 1970. Night shift
comes through the looking-glass walls of the airport cafe.
Branniff and United Airlines roar out of sight to exotic places.
Somewhere a radio blasts Leon Russell singing *". . . here comes
Uncle Sam again with the same old bag of beans. Local chiefs on the
radio, we got some hungry mouths to feed, goin' back to Alcatraz."*

At 6:30 P.M., one hundred Vietnam draftees drag into the
Oklahoma City airport cafe. Afros, pork-chop sideburns, crew
cuts, Indian braids. After two years, hairless pimpled faces all
look alike. Some smell bad. Some have beautiful teeth.

It's not news at the airport cafe that the Vietnam War is
being fought disproportionately by the poor. Every Monday
through Friday we serve red and yellow, black, and poor white
boys their last suppers as civilians. They're on their way to boot
camp. They clutch their government orders and puke-belch
to themselves. Their hands shake. My hands are steady. I want
to tell them to run. But don't.

*"No one gets hurt if they do what they're told," whispered the
white teacher through the door of the broom closet. "Would you like
to come out now?"*

"Curious," booms a voice across the airport cafe's dining room.
Some of the draftees look toward the kitchen, others continue
eating as if they'd heard nothing.

The voice gathers strength and explodes.

"There were no survivors of Babi Yar," roars Gretchen grimly.

I rush through the kitchen door. The steaks are burning,
and the beans are boiling over the fire, and Gretchen is scruti-
nizing Nina in front of the gas grill.

"Your story is certainly unfamiliar to me. You probably
branded your own thumb so people won't accuse you. Very
clever."

Nina's eyes make a circle of the kitchen. She examines her

work: the stainless steel bins of freshly washed lettuce, toma-
toes, radish flowers, onions, carrots, and watermelon balls. All
are arranged, lined up in neat rows at her workstation. "I do
what I am told," she says pushing her head against the walk-in
freezer. "The sins of my occupation."

"What a wreck you are. Always building a pile of shadows,"
says Gretchen, grabbing a slice of onion.

Nina's mouth is set in a fold of bitterness. "I know Babi Yar.
It's a ravine near Kiev where the Germans murdered thirty-five
thousand Jews in September 1941. By 1943, it had become a
mass grave for more than a hundred thousand Jews." She looks
at something beyond us, then screams. "I WAS THERE!"

"Yes, but what did you do?"

Nina charges Gretchen with a butcher knife in one hand
and a watermelon scoop in the other. Gretchen holds a small
toaster oven in front of her like a shield. Together they dance
around the room like a couple of marionettes being pulled by
the fingers of God.

Eventually Susan B. Anthony interrupts the madness and
Gretchen shouts, "SCHWEIG, du Neger!"

This is where I come in. I intercede like a good union steward should. Susan B. Anthony holds a hot pan of grease and is
set to attack them both. The World War II survivors are screaming in languages I can't understand and pointing their weapons.
They all scare the hell out of me because I'm unarmed.

1970 is a terrible year to be a teenage Indian in Oklahoma
City. Vietnam is on television nightly. World War II is still
going on in the kitchen of the airport cafe, and I'm losing my
classmates to mortar fire in Asia. Emmet Tahbone is dead. Blown
away, literally. Richard Warrior is MIA, and George Billy has a
shrapnel mouth.

This past week there were sit-ins at a downtown department store where blacks are still being refused service at the
lunch counter. For almost ten months American Indians have

occupied the abandoned prison on Alcatraz Island. The word on the streets of Oklahoma City is that we're fed up with colonialism. American Indians are finally going to change the status quo. Standing in the middle of the kitchen with my palms turned upward, a sign that I carry no weapons, I squint like a mourner who draws the curtains against the light. I feel powerless to change anything.

I look out the window and a moonbeam is crisscrossing a watery plain. It's the Pearl River with its saw grass islands and cypress knees rising out of the water like hands in prayer to Hashtali, whose eye is the Sun. This light once cut clear across the heavens and down to the Choctaws' ancient mother mound, the Nanih Waiya in the Lower Mississippi Valley. Now it's no longer visible except on special occasions.

I see a Choctaw woman, her daughter, and their relatives. They're being attacked by a swarm of warriors from another tribe. Unfortunately bad weather has driven them into a little bayou. They're exposed from head to foot to their enemies, the Cherokees, who've been following them for days. The Choctaw woman shows her daughter how to be brave. Several times she runs and cuts the powder horns loose from her dead relatives in order to distribute them among the living. Finally the seven warriors, and the mother and daughter, seeing that they can no longer hold their ground, rush headlong upon their enemies.

A feminine voice interrupts my vision. *"No one gets hurt if they do what they're told."* I shake my head, trying to drive it out of me. *"We fly daily nonstop flights to locations across America, Europe, and Asia,"* continues the recorded message on the airport's loudspeaker.

I turn back to my co-workers, who are drowning in a pool of tears. "No one will get hurt if we do what we're supposed to do," I say meekly. For a moment no one moves. Then they begin struggling with their kitchen utensils. Suddenly Nina is composed, Gretchen too; both of them square their shoulders the

way soldiers do when called to attention. They promise it will
never happen again, but no one believes them.

At midnight the lines on my face have melted like the clock
in Salvador Dali's painting. I resemble a sad clown. When Susan
B. Anthony and I walk outside to share a smoke we eye one
other wearily.

"What happened?" I ask quietly.

"God knows," she says, lighting a cigarette.

Together we watch as the lights of a crayon-colored Branniff
jet leave a trail of stale dead air, and I think I'll buy a mask and
become someone else. The AFL-CIO can't save me now.

Choctalking on Other Realities

I did become someone else. A mother, a teacher, a writer, a wife.
When the opportunity came to visit Israel in 1992, I signed up
for the two-week trip at the behest of my husband, a geographer
and co-leader of the study tour. We are going to Jerusalem
to learn about the effects of the Intifada on the region and
its peoples. At first, I was hesitant. The very name Jerusalem
connotes religion. Three of them: Judaism, Christianity, Islam,
birthed in that order. They all look the same to me. They share
one God known as Yahweh, Allah, or Jesus. They honor the
same prophets. They share many of the same books. Their holidays center around religious and cultural victories over each
other. Kind of like Americans celebrating Thanksgiving. Holidays
are the masks of conquerors.

But wouldn't you know it. On my first day in Jerusalem
I met a Jewish woman who said her great-grandmother was
a Cherokee.

She tells me it is a long story—how one side of her family
immigrated to America, then re-immigrated to Israel after 1948.
I stand motionless and look at the woman across the glass
counter of her gift shop. Listen skeptically to the ragged tender-
ness of her story. The weary but elusive Indian ancestry, the

fawning desire to be related to me, at least to my Indianness, is something I've experienced before.

I study the shopkeeper's face. We are remarkably alike. Black eyes. Dark hair. About the same age. As the shadows of Jerusalem invade her shop windows I grow nostalgic. The city looms under a delicious haze of smoke from the outdoor falafel stands, and I want to take this woman away with me. To cross time and the ocean together. To place her in our past, to put myself in her beginning, and intertwine our threads of history— for we are nothing without our relationships. That's Choctaw.

I begin my story in the middle. "Choctaws are not originally from Oklahoma. We are immigrants too."

The woman whose ancestor was a Cherokee nods her head as if she understands, and I continue.

"Our ancient homelands are in the southeastern part of the United States where we were created in the spectacular silken flatness of the delta lands. The earth opened her body and beckoned us to join her above ground, so our ancestors tunneled up through her navel into tinges of moist red men and women. We collected our chins, knees, breasts, and sure-footed determination—long before Moses parted the Red Sea, and the God with three heads was born in the Middle East.

"Choctaws were the second largest allied group of peoples in the Southeast. Our population centers were clustered like wheels around three major rivers: to the east the Tombigbee River; to the west the Pearl River; and in the South the Chicka-sawhay River. We made trading relationships with other tribes in our regions whenever possible."

She interrupts my story, asks me if I will come to her house for an evening meal. She talks on. Says that she went to school in New York City, and that she misses the company of Americans. Her own mother is dead, since she was a child. All she has left is her father, the one who owns the shop. She looks at me. "You promise to tell me more of your history?"

"What I can."

Her home is west of Jerusalem. Opposite the Old City where everyone walks instead of rides. There are great American-style streets full of Mercedes, Peugeots, and Perrier bottles. Her place is elegant, an estate on a hill. There's a dark studio with a mahogany desk, Navajo rugs, and an enormous basket made from the skeleton of a Saguaro tree sits near the stone fireplace. She builds a fire against the cold and opens the shutters to let in the city. She says she doesn't feel anything in particular toward the Arabs, no hate, no revulsion either. I asked her what about the Choctaws? She smiles, not knowing what I mean. She says she is where she has to be. Placed here. Of course she feels a tinge of fear. It's as if this is not only what she expects, but what must happen to her.

She says she pays closest attention to the noise of the city. That the city shouts what is going to happen. The explosions, the bullets, the prayers, the celebratory demonstrations, they're all part of it, she says, like messages from God.

She begins telling me some rigmarole about how Jerusalem meets the needs of all its people. Throughout its four-thousand-year history, she says, the city was meant to be a place of unity. Her father believes that now the Intifada is over, there can be peace between the Arabs and Jews.

Behind her a shadow walks into the room. I see the image of a woman in darned socks. I think I recognize her face, but I can't quite make it out, so I speak up without waiting for a polite pause in our conversation.

"Then why, every day, do Jews and Arabs try and kill one another?"

"Why did Indians sell Manhattan to the Christians?"

Night comes through the shutters. The din of the streets below grows louder. It's more penetrating than the livid red streetlamps.

We look at each other. Our expressions are suddenly

changed. We realize we're on the side of societies that have reduced us to grief.

All the same she rushes to tell me the story of her great-grandfather, a shoemaker, an outcast in North Carolina just like her great-grandmother, the Cherokee. "He was in exile, she was conquered. They fell in love because they had this in common. After World War II my grandfather, the one who was half-Jewish-half-Cherokee, made a pilgrimage to the Holy Land. He never returned to America."

"Indians are not conquered!"

"But your nerve is gone," she says, sadly. "I was a student at New York City University when the Indians surrendered Alcatraz Island in June 1971. We would have never given up."

There is a long silence.

"Who is we?" I ask.

"I've provoked you," she says. "Now I give you the chance to give me a piece of your mind."

There was a trace of something odd in her remark, so I began with a metaphor. "Once a very ancient god came back from everywhere. Arriving at a banquet in his honor with a bundle of keys, he announced that it was closing time, and toilets around the world exploded."

We laugh. It breaks the tension.

"It's from the Good Book. The missing pages."

"And then what happened?" she asks. "You promised to tell me your history."

"After the war ended between the British and the French in 1763, Indians in the Southeast couldn't make the foreigners do anything. Soldiers went AWOL and married into our tribes. No one wanted to live in Paris or London anymore. That's why so many Choctaws, Creeks, Chickasaws, and Cherokees have British and French last names.

"In 1830, after the Treaty of Dancing Rabbit Creek was signed, the Choctaws were the first to be removed from our ancient homelands. Many walked all the way with very little to eat or drink. The road to the Promised Land was terrible. Dead horses and their dead riders littered the way. Dead women lay in the road with babies dried to their breasts, tranquil as if napping. A sacred compost for scavengers."

She stokes the fire to keep it from dying, and I know the more revolting the details, the less she believes me. Finally she says. "You are exaggerating."

"Perhaps. But four thousand Choctaws died immigrating to Oklahoma."

"It is late," she says, ignoring my facts. "Time I returned you to your hotel. I'm sure your husband is waiting for you."

"But you said you wanted to know about my history?"

She gives me a fishy look but agrees. "Very well."

"It's no accident that there are sixty-six Indian nations headquartered in Oklahoma. Oklahoma or Indian Territory was a forerunner of Israel. Choctaws were the first to be removed there; other Indian tribes from around country soon followed. We were supposed live together in peace. Form relationships. It wasn't easy, but for the most part we did it because we do not idealize war. However, throughout the nineteenth century more and more whites moved into Indian territory. Followed by missionaries and lawyers who began converting us, or swindling us."

"Then on April 22, 1889 the American government opened the unassigned lands to the whites. When the trumpet sounded, the Run of 1889 began. It was estimated that twenty thousand immigrants were waiting at the border to stake their claims. Today the Run of 1889 is an annual celebration in Oklahoma. Like a holiday."

"I thought you were going to tell me *your* story."

"I'm coming to it," I answer, pausing to clear my throat. "There was no color in the broom closet. Light edged around the door. There may have been other teachers outside the closet, but I only knew of her by the smell of her sweat.

"The church had started a kindergarten program. She was a missionary. That morning the preacher said we were lucky to have a missionary lead us in a song. *"Red and yellow, black and white we are separate in his sight, Jesus loves the little children of the world."* Then I sang it several times by myself. I was only repeating what I thought I heard. The words had no meaning for me; I was five years old. When she marched toward me shaking her fist, with that mouth of angry nails, I panicked and ran outside across the playground and toward a cafe.

"Down, down, down, the fall crushes me, and I'm mucking around in the dirt. She oozed through my pores that hot afternoon in Bethany Oklahoma, and there she has remained whispering inside my head."

I stare at my host. "It isn't that we lost our nerve. Sometimes we're just overwhelmed."

After I finished my story, a strange quiet grips the Jewish woman whose ancestor was a Cherokee. Her face becomes attentive, as if listening to something that penetrated her soul.

When she drops me off at the National Palace Hotel, I watch her drive away. All I can think of is that she's right, that Jerusalem, "the city of peace," is what is meant to happen to her.

I Learn There Is No God But God

The next day I rejoin our study tour and we meet some Palestinian women from the Gaza Strip. In 1992 the Gaza Strip is still one of the Occupied Territories of Israel. The Palestinian women tell us stories of their lives through an interpreter. One woman says that the government prohibits them from displaying the colors of the Palestinian flag, which are green, red, black, and white. She says her husband has been arrested for having a picture of a watermelon on his desk. Many others show us empty tear-gas canisters that have been shot into their homes by the soldiers. They are plainly marked MADE IN USA.

To show concern for the Palestinians some members of our

study tour present the women with duffel bags full of used clothes and high-heeled shoes marked MADE IN USA. I didn't bring any used clothes, so I ask the Christian coordinator from the Council of Middle East Churches if I could give the Palestinian women money instead of used clothes.

"No," she replies. "They'll just come to expect it from us."

The next day when the study tour leaves for a two-day visit for Nazareth, I stay behind at our hotel. I've had enough. I want to be alone, walk the streets of the Old City, and eat in the small cafes.

Throughout the day prayers are broadcast over loud speakers. For Muslims, the first prayer of the day begins at the moment the rays of the sun begin to appear on the horizon. The last prayer in the evening ends at sunset. Devout Jews pray three times a day; devout Muslims pray five times daily. When I hear a man singing the prayers on a mosque's loudspeaker system I am sure he is praying to the Sun, just like Choctaws once prayed to Hashtali.

"The prayers are to Allah, not the Sun," says a vendor outside the Al-Aqsa Mosque in Jerusalem.

"It looks like you are praying to the Sun, especially with your palms turned up toward the sky. The Egyptians once worshipped the Sun God, Ra. Since the Hebrews and the Egyptians once lived together, maybe your religions rubbed off on each other. Everyone in this country says 'Yis-RA-el' for Israel. Maybe there's a relationship?"

He waved me away. "No, no, no, you have been misinformed! There is no God but the God of us all."

I Am Still Running

Palestinian men from around the community race past me toward the soldiers and meet them head-on. The protest explodes into a riot. Mothers, daughters, and grandmothers from inside the shops join the women in the streets. The soldiers begin dragging people inside the blue and white paddy wagons, one or two at a time, amidst weeping and bleeding fists.

I run toward the leader crumpled against a stone wall and recognize her. It's Nina from the airport cafe. I can't believe it, but it's really Nina. She is dressed in her white cotton uniform, her shabby socks still held up with rubber bands. A soldier reaches her before me.

"Don't hurt her, it's Nina. Can't you see? She's a survivor of Babi Yar."

Suddenly I'm on the ground. I cannot breathe. Someone rifles through my purse and pulls out my American passport. He yanks me up by my arms and tells me in English to go home.

No one gets hurt if they do what they're told.

"No, it's a lie. RUN!" I scream so loud that I frighten the voice out of my head.

Nina gets up and tries to jump the stone fence, but the soldier bashes her in the legs with a club. She falls down and he carries her to the paddy wagon and shoves her inside.

I am back to the dubious place where memory distorts fragments of an indivisible experience and we meet a different self. It wasn't Nina the soldier carried into the government vehicle. She died talking to God that terrible night in the airport cafe. She collapsed on the floor of the kitchen, not long after the fight with Gretchen, asking God why she had to die, why now that she'd regained her courage. "Very well," was all she whispered.

Standing in the middle of the street in East Jerusalem, I watch the determined faces of the Palestinian women and weep for Nina. I still believe she is with the Palestinian protesters, just as I believe she was at Babi Yar.

An Arab member of the Knesset, the Israeli parliament, finally arrives in a government car and calls for calm. He holds both hands out to the soldiers, a sign that he carries no weapons.

The pigeon returns and lands next to me, as if surveying the waste. The Knesset member sees us, stops, then walks on with

his palms facing toward the Sun. I will believe the rest of
my life that this is what he prayed for.

"Save her. She is the Jewish women shot to death by the
Germans at Babi Yar.

"Save her. She is the Palestinian women shot to death
by the Jews at Deir Yassin.

"Save her. She is the Vietnamese women shot to death
by the Americans at My Lai.

"Save her. She is the Mayan women shot to death by the
Mexicans in Chiapas.

"Save her. She is the Black women shot to death by the
Ku Klux Klan in Alabama.

"Save her. She is The People, our grandmothers, our mothers,
our sisters, our ancestors, ourselves.

"Save us."

Linda Noel » Konkow Maidu

Stitch upon Stitch
For Lisa

She brings new breath
Through all of us
To start the winter with

Precious circles
In the motion
Of her beginnings
Which bares
Our own birth
In basket stitch belief
Born again and again
In the first breath
Of her birth
From her father's thigh
Bursting into
The spark within
Her mother's belly cave
Which breathes blood
Into all of our circles
Stitched with sun
And buzzard wing
Bending sky designs
Pushed from between
Woman legs
Another stitch
Pushed through sky
Pressed through lifting
Geese wings

Suzanne Rancourt » Abenaki

Sipping

for my mother

It was not always bone china, the cup
the saucer, that your long feathered fingered hands wrapped
and chipped as flakes of teeth tunked by the mouth
of a beer bottle: the cup, the saucer, holding
the moisture of an eggshell candling its paper-porcelainness
to count your shadowed maybes on the other side,
like in the old days when kerosene rags haloed your brow
of buggy locks. It only smelt as bad as it was.

No one really believed

the stories of clothing fashioned burlap from sugar,
flour, or potato sacks or that the lamb
really hung itself and its mother bleated for it
for days, her tits festered with grief that you
still added to your tea and stirred with a sterling
spoon with some unknown initial bought with
bottle money at a high-end junk shop because you
could finally do that but no one really believed
the pastoral truth of poverty and trudging for miles
to a colder school than the walk through snowdrifts
or the belly-down-face-first sled ride past Springers
not the toboggan ride that broke your leg. You knew
no one had a spirit like yours. But no one
really believed it anymore than the sound of silent
precision of breath and the polyrhythms of chomping bits
and restless hooves while hitching up the team of horses
to the sleigh, buffalo lap blankets and all those
brass bells—gold gilt, brass bells, gold
rimmed your post-menopausal Currier and Ives
teacups chattering on trays accompanied by

different spoons but still silver and embossed. Com'boss!
Com'boss! And who's boss on the farm
whose soil milked sweat and youth from the backs of boys,
their spines a stack of wafers: no more Canadian jigs.
All compressed into a bale of square-cornered hay
and stacks of photo albums and things you wanted to be
when you had enough desire to dream and hope.

Who could have guessed?

No more switchel no more swinging scythe
no more Jimmy Stewart hay rides, no more no
more all in one square-cornered hay a kachunking machine
pursed forth a cube of nutrition, ready the black tea,
render the recollections of bitterness that you could not
set down:

Squirrels no longer fascinate me nor do people sitting
in parks or at city bus stops. Joggers
have become commonplace as the knee pads
on rollerbladers, or headphones, cell phones and
microfiber. But nobody believes me either.

Who'd believe you'd die?

Only the tea
tastes good piping hot from copper kettles,
mine is black, no English twist of milk,
just dark amber that only stark post-menopausal bone
china can appreciate with a tinkling curiosity
of what if's and sugar cubes the size of croutons
molasses tan and irregular like brown eggs
brought in from under the hen's ass in a child's hands
cradling the process before bigger hands crack it all

and somewhere between the delicate bird bites
of fresh bread and raspberry preserves the squeal
of a stuck pig became a seed betwixt your teeth and lard
on the palate your tongue dabbed unconsciously
and repeatedly painting on your retina the
goofiness of horror:
a barking shadow-dog on a canvas tent wall,
the neighbor girl and her baby as they died
in a head-on collision. Who'd have guessed it was you
driving behind them and witnessed
the explosive ball of white light a microsecond
prior to impact.
Sitting alone with a cup of tea was almost too much.

Whatever Greek poet said a heifer could be milked
was just damn wrong and no matter how you mixed it
the lamb still hung itself and you ate it.

One at a Time

Autumn 1997, for Angelito

"There is a hunger for order
but a thirst against."
—Linda Gregg

1
Two crisp sunflowers are small enough
and will fit into the weave
of your palm-size casket.

I am pouring you into water.
The equinox, midwifery
and practical herbs
unraveling the flesh between us.
I felt you
and still
you enclose me.
I bargain with God for a reversal.
Life's fragility, the inflexible end
excessive.

The small altar on the counter.
Votives hover around me,
my body is an apparition, hermetic,
like you, just that far
off from my grasp. You
go through me everywhere.
I say you
will pass beyond in four days.

2

I herd goats from the crisp corn field.
June's last planting, they munch the fodder,
carefully eyeing me, unwilling to be stopped,
though I was competent.
They saw my stick
and turned tail,
straight to their corral.
They look at me,
pissed, but put up with it.

The strain in my pelvis became hard
after the hog's regular feeding.
Getting him fattened
for a spring slaughter.

I walk a different path back,

notice a familiar scent—the astringent stamen,
the red vulvas in the season's devil claws
releasing their love-juice
for the pollinators. A cluster
eaten out bare
by a moth's tenacious mouth.

Entering, and re-entering.
All the world shifts.
I bend to draw in their scent,
press my face into their pollen.
Their scent is on me
and I back up
nearly falling to the ground,
pluck a handful and rush away.

The bugles of a tobacco tree
trumpet a faded yellow song. I follow a worn path
to the house, gather new corn pollen,
elder going to berry.

3

All the candles in the house self-extinguish.
The ones from Mexico, hand-painted "Tu y Yo,"
the last ones to go out,
tiny wicks curling under the clear pool of wax . . .
My husband asks are you ready?
we walk onto the moist ground
he prepares for the ceremony.

You are sacred,
this life we gave you
taken.

I pull on a chair to stand.
The tremor in my body
like an unraveling rope
that gets away
no matter where my hands grasp.
Me, you, his eyes, his look.
I know again

how awful this becomes.
He looks up at sky,
a weightless altar,
the sun a witness to what happens,
and I don't feel better,
cedar, the eagle feather, the prayers
don't stop this shriveling,
this anger, this fist I've become.

Term

The moon of my stomach,
curved wide and round
catches what its wants—
the moon's pale light.
She sees her body here.

Nothing ever stops
not living or dead.

At the ninth new moon
tough, winding kicks
and strumming on my ribs . . .
like a call to one more gradual death.

Inside I'm on the verge,
the place of nowhere else
but out,
the child's exchange
of water for air.

Next to me my man-raven,
his strands of steel-blue light.
I touch their fragile glow
without waking child or man.

I am every noise
before dawn's lips
suck in the dew
of a late monsoon.

Moon stomach, rolling,
heavy movement.

Life of me, of him, of moonlight.

There is nothing else I feel
except the pulling weight.

Eating then sleep, there's
more to you than me.
Pressing your head hard
smoothing the muscle
the sacred passageway
to the above world.

Until her tenth face, night's pale eye,
surfaces again.

Your motion, beyond what skin can give.
And him, his smooth slope of hip
I want to swallow, want this moment still,

to shed the mammoth
allow time to kiss tenderly my wounds,
and open again, tentatively . . .
just one body,
to his.

» » »

Limp Strings

I am driving home, the weekend ahead
planting garlic and grading freshman essays
on the brain.Did he get to the dishes, or
are they piled to greet me. Milpa cries,
her mouth's wet rim quivers, echoes
my jangled pessimism, a wicked necklace,
the O of her mouth comes to me fast before the blur
of my neighbor's field of alfalfa and sky.
I try not to swerve while my fingers
snatch the buckles on her overalls,
her face bobs like a doll loose at its hinges.
My knee steers and, the stick popped in neutral,
I pull her from the arm-joint—
a fast look to the road, lift and remove her
from the second-hand car seat.

Think: most accidents happen within a mile or two of home.
Something I read in a doctor's office.
Thrust her toward me one more time
under the wheel, buttons unfastened.
Rose-lips root around my breast,
her free hand considers the other nipple.

Flutter in her feet,
her fingers pinch hard,
stretch the dark nipple,
until it goes numb, then crisp . . . .

I see myself like a *Mad* magazine caricature,
a devotion to distorted bodies.
When telling stories, I refer to my boobs
as two long and limp strings,

to cheer myself.
If I didn't wear a shirt to conceal them
they would flap like shoe-strings
in the monsoon winds of August;
My husband hears and watches me say this.
Rolls his eyes.
He likes his flapjacks.

Karenne Wood » Monacan

Red Hawk Woman

in memory of Thomasina Jordan

Now you are among us and now gone the way light
diffuses through forest and only remembers the sun.

Now you are red sky woman who sets fires to paint the clouds.
Now you are white breath woman rising through mountains
    at dawn.

Now you are yellow pollen woman who gives birth
    to blossoming plants.
Now you are black night woman with eyes that grow round
    in the dark.

We have seen death in its gracious and varied shapes
    all this time.
We saw battles where the best of us fell, and we cried
    for ourselves.

You remembered in us a wisdom that flows with the blood,
    courage
to leave the grief we recalled for the grief we cannot yet imagine.

You led us into Washington, that city of bones, where we spoke
with earnest words the dreams our ancestors wished into us.

Now we give you back to the green skin of earth and here
lay down the quarrels and obsessions that weaken us all.

Now we take up your life in our hands and walk together,
our prayers the simplest act of remembrance.

O, Native woman wearing the songs of ten thousand
years in your hair, who among us is like you?

Walk with us through the darkness where we arm ourselves
knowing it was not dying you taught us to do.

Evangeline Parsons Yazzie » Navajo

Vicks

"Mom, my legs hurt!"

"Oh those are just growing pains. Go get the Vicks and rub some on your legs, then your legs will grow slower and that way they won't hurt as much." With a healthy dose of Vicks on our legs, we would go back outside and play some more. Hours later, we'd come in with dirt and Vicks plastered on our legs. Perhaps that is why our beds always had so much sand in them.

"Mom, my head hurts."

"Well, go get the Vicks and rub some on your forehead, around your ears, and inside your nose, and go to sleep. You'll feel better when you wake up." It seemed I did go to sleep a lot sooner with Vicks on my forehead, on the ears, and inside my nostrils.

"Mom, my eyes are red and they hurt."

"Just get the Vicks and rub it on your eyelids. It may sting at first, but that will go away." I would walk around in the kitchen squinting for a while because the Vicks was working.

"Mom, daddy's elbows are chap! It hurts when his elbow rubs against my arm as he is driving."

"Here, I have some Vicks, put several coats on his elbow so that the chapped area will not turn dark, and people will not notice his chapped elbows."

"Mom, my throat hurts."

"Go gargle with salt water and put some Vicks on your neck then wrap one of your father's old T-shirts around your neck. Put some Vicks on your chest too, that way you won't cough and get your throat more sore."

"Don't let me forget to get another jar of Vicks, the next time we go to town."

"Did you get me a bottle of Vicks, like I told you to?"

"Yes, it's right here in the bag."

"I told you to get me a jar of Vicks, not Mentholatum! This Mentholatum is too greasy!"

Did my mother just like the smell of Vicks or what?

2 *Strong Hearts*

In this section you will find poems and prose that are at once political and personal: poems to fallen women warriors such as Lorena Fuerta's tribute to murdered American Indian activist Anna Mae Aquash, to fallen brother warriors whose lives, even if on the street or at the margins, we must honor, even avenge. In the words here we find, as in Inés Hernández-Avila's "Tough Audience," that "Indi'n women are tough / we can see through things, / people, situations, games, / and cut to the heart of it all." Poems like Laura Tohe's "In Dinétah" and Karenne Wood's "In Memory of Shame" do cut to that heart of it all, cut us to the heart as they chant us through the universal pain of war (war on Natives, world war, war on women) to the way of beauty that will save us.

We organized this section around the notion of strength, the strength of bone and of that most powerful muscle in our bodies, the heart. And yet, in reflecting on one of the stories in this section, Laura wrote, "While we often speak of celebrating women's traditions and perseverance, there is much to say about the complexities of how women's strength can turn abusive. We see this in Auntie in [Leslie Marmon] Silko's *Ceremony*. We see it again in Haaland's 'Mother's Love.' Still, the narrator, overcome by love and honor, defends her mother in this moving narrative of abuse and cruelty."

Laura also recognized the way in which our relatedness is our strength when she wrote in her introduction to the first section of this anthology, "It is often the women who form the backbone of their nations. " I recall that when Laura and I began discussing what we saw as a common thread in the work we had chosen, we talked of how women's words and works uphold nations. Laura mentioned the saying, "A nation is not lost until its women's hearts are on the ground." These writings show hearts held above the ground, nations held up by strong women.

My cousin Ramona once ran an organization to prevent community violence called Strong Hearts of the Circle. She based the idea for her program on one of the Dakota warrior societies. Traditionally, members of the Strong Hearts were the most brave, those whose feats in battle served to protect the people. The name Strong Hearts seems to me an honor to warriors, male or female, who use the strengths of the human heart—encouragement, endurance, compassion—to uphold and protect the nations.

The women whose writings are contained in this section form a new, literary Strong Hearts society. To be a Strong Heart, these writings reveal, means to be brave, to take courage into your heart, to let love be your shield and if need be, your weapon.

Heid E. Erdrich

A Cousin from California Shows Up at My House, The First Time in Thirty Years

At ten he obeyed the laws of gravity
on raw ponies heading for the open road,
pandered to a doting gramma's cultured silence
and held his breath when border town cops
in slow motion stopped his father's weaving car.
Flashing lights. Lyric beauty frame by frame.
Grim passages of deadly games became
the telltale snare of tantalizing curiosity.

At twenty-something, in crisp wartime whites
he watched a blonde girl running with her dog
in the streets of one of those base cities and thought
of kids running in all directions, like himself; he left
on a ship for hostile waters, every echo
in the fog a reminder that he was far from home.

At middle age now he wants to read what he
might have written, the words of a woman
cousin who believes herself to be a poet.
She reminds him of how it was at Bowed Head's Place
where they both grew up, hardly speaking,
neither confiding in the other. All afternoon he
turns the pages. The twilight sounds of summer birds
seem to mirror the sounds of stories untold and real.
He didn't know. He didn't know. How to talk
of precious moments.

There are still Dakotahs growing up tribal
on the Crow Creek not forgetting anything;
They go about their lives on the theory
that the world is exactly as it is perceived.

Susan Deer Cloud ⊚ Mohawk/Blackfeet

Doe Season

Unexpected snow this morning. She opened her eyes
thinking it must be Christmas Day, but it was still November.
Already she could hear guns blasting open the woods' watchful
silence, bullets burning through fur, flesh, spattering blood
on fearful snow. She hated doe season. She wondered
if any hunters, swaddled in bright orange so they wouldn't be
shot themselves, ever offered a prayer of thanks to the deer
whose lives they stole. Long ago her Mohawk great-grandfathers
thanked their four-legged sisters for relinquishing their bodies
as food for the frozen moons to come. And once she told
    her nephews
they, too, should offer thanks to slain doe.

So much was lost. Shuddering against cold as the bare trees
outside shivered against pale sky, she slipped into her thick robe,
    descending the stairs to the kitchen. She spotted deer tracks
by the house where her lover had tossed apples, tried to entice
does to stay in the sanctuary of their backyard. "Ghosts,"
    she thought, making Eight O'Clock drip coffee in the old
    aluminum pot
her father once used, its smell swelling slowly to fill the
yellow-walled room with bitter-sweet. On the porch
glass wind chimes clanked close to shattering, juncos flying up
in a furious swirl of snow flurries, a mad north wind. "I can't
    stand this weather," her lover groaned, his eyes the color
    of coffee grounds, his sun-hungry face sunk with ghosts.
    Pouring their coffee, silently she offered him up a prayer
    of thanks for not hunting doe.

What was it her mother used to say about ghosts? Some remark
about how the older she got the more ghosts inhabited
her body, the older she grew the more her body became

like a haunted house. Now her dead mother was one of many
ghosts inside her *own* body. She had done what daughters are
    warned they'll do—turned into her mother, drinking coffee,
    dreaming through glass. Beyond the sliding door she could
    see the past
piled up like accidental snow, snow she would have to tread
doe-like paths through. She dreamed of the last hunting season
she endured with her ex-husband, the night he ribbed
    a barroom buddy
about a doe he'd shot. "How could you shoot any *thing* as pretty
    as her through the heart?" her ex asked. "Me, I only kill
    the ugly ones"—speaking of doe as if they were women,
    laughing, spilling beer on his blood-red jacket, doe permit
    pinned to its back. She parted from him before the next
    day's sun shot across the mountain tops.

Unexpected snow this morning—gun blasts in the forest,
men hunting doe, other men hunting women, threatening them
with guns, some shooting the ones they decide are ugly,
some murdering even the prettiest ones.

Louise Erdrich ◉ Ojibwe

The Shawl

Among the Anishinaabeg on the road where I live, it is told how a woman loved a man other than her husband and went off into the bush and bore his child. Her name was Aanakwad, which means cloud, and like a cloud she was changeable. She was moody and sullen one moment, her lower lip jutting and her eyes flashing, filled with storms. The next, she would shake her hair over her face and blow it straight out in front of her to make her children scream with laughter. For she also had two children by her husband, one a yearning boy of five years and the other a capable daughter of nine.

When Aanakwad brought the new baby out of the trees that autumn, the older girl was like a second mother, even waking in the night to clean the baby and nudge it to her mother's breast. Aanakwad slept through its cries, hardly woke. It wasn't that she didn't love her baby; no, it was the opposite—she loved it too much, the way she loved its father, and not her husband. This passion ate away at her, and her feelings were unbearable. If she could have thrown off that wronghearted love, she would have, but the thought of the other man, who lived across the lake, was with her always. She became a gray sky, stared monotonously at the walls, sometimes wept into her hands for hours at a time. Soon, she couldn't rise to cook or keep the cabin neat, and it was too much for the girl, who curled up each night exhausted in her red-and-brown plaid shawl, and slept and slept, until the husband had to wake her to awaken her mother, for he was afraid of his wife's bad temper, and it was he who roused Aanakwad into anger by the sheer fact that he was himself and not the other.

At last, even though he loved Aanakwad, the husband had to admit that their life together was no good anymore. And it was he who sent for the other man's uncle. In those days, our people lived widely scattered, even out on the plains. There were no roads then, just trails, though we had horses and wagons and, for the winter, sleds. When the uncle came around to fetch Aanakwad, in his wagon fitted out with sled runners, it was very hard, for she and her husband had argued right up to the last about the children, argued fiercely until the husband had finally given in. He turned his face to the wall, and did not move to see the daughter, whom he treasured, sit down beside her mother, wrapped in her plaid robe in the wagon bed. They left right away, with their bundles and sacks, not bothering to heat up the stones to warm their feet. The father had stopped his ears, so he did not hear his son cry out when he suddenly understood that he would be left behind.

As the uncle slapped the reins and the horse lurched forward, the boy tried to jump into the wagon, but his mother pried his hands off the boards, crying, *Gego, gego,* and he fell down hard. But there was something in him that would not let her leave. He jumped up and, although he was wearing only light clothing, he ran behind the wagon over the packed drifts. The horses picked up speed. His chest was scorched with pain, and yet he pushed himself on. He'd never run so fast, so hard and furiously, but he was determined, and he refused to believe that the increasing distance between him and the wagon was real. He kept going until his throat closed, he saw red, and in the ice of the air his lungs shut. Then, as he fell onto the board-hard snow, he raised his head. He watched the back of the wagon and the tiny figures of his mother and sister disappear, and something failed in him. Something broke. At that moment he truly did not care if he was alive or dead. So when he saw the gray shapes, the shadows, bounding lightly from the trees to either side of the trail, far ahead, he was not afraid.

The next the boy knew, his father had wrapped him in a blanket and was carrying him home. His father's chest was broad and, although he already spat the tubercular blood that would write the end of his story, he was still a strong man. It would take many years to die. In those years, the father would tell the boy, who had forgotten this part entirely, that at first when he talked about the shadows the father thought he'd been visited by *manidoog*. But then, as the boy described the shapes, his father had understood that they were not spirits. Uneasy, he had decided to take his gun back along the trail. He had built up the fire in the cabin, and settled his boy near it, and gone back out into the snow. Perhaps the story spread through our settlements because the father had to tell what he saw, again and again, in order to get rid of it. Perhaps as with all frightful dreams, *amaniso,* he had to talk about it to destroy its power—though in this case nothing could stop the dream from being real.

The shadows' tracks were the tracks of wolves, and in those days, when our guns had taken all their food for furs and hides to sell, the wolves were bold and had abandoned the old agreement between them and the first humans. For a time, until we understood and let the game increase, the wolves hunted us. The father bounded forward when he saw the tracks. He could see where the pack, desperate, had tried to slash the tendons of the horses' legs. Next, where they'd leaped for the back of the wagon. He hurried on to where the trail gave out at the broad empty ice of the lake. There, he saw what he saw, scattered, and the ravens, attending to the bitter small leavings of the wolves.

For a time, the boy had no understanding of what had happened. His father kept what he knew to himself, at least that first year, and when his son asked about his sister's torn plaid shawl, and why it was kept in the house, his father said nothing. But he wept when the boy asked if his sister was cold. It was only after his father had been weakened by the disease that he began to tell the story, far too often and always the same way: he told how when the wolves closed in, Aanakwad had thrown her daughter to them.

When his father said those words, the boy went still. What had his sister felt? What had thrust through her heart? Had something broken inside her, too, as it had in him? Even then, he knew that this broken place inside him would not be mended, except by some terrible means. For he kept seeing his mother put the baby down and grip his sister around the waist. He saw Aanakwad swing the girl lightly out over the side of the wagon. He saw the brown shawl with its red lines flying open. He saw the shadows, the wolves, rush together, quick and avid, as the wagon with sled runners disappeared into the distance—forever, for neither he nor his father saw Aanakwad again.

When I was little, my own father terrified us with his drinking. This was after we lost our mother, because before that the only time I was aware that he touched the *ishkode waaboo* was on an occasional weekend when they got home late, or sometimes during berry-picking gatherings when we went out to the bush and camped with others. Not until she died did he start the heavy sort of drinking, the continuous drinking, where we were left alone in the house for days. The kind where, when he came home, we'd jump out the window and hide in the woods while he barged around, shouting for us. We'd go back only after he had fallen dead asleep.

There were three of us: me, the oldest at ten, and my little sister and brother, twins, and only six years old. I was surprisingly good at taking care of them, I think, and because we learned to survive together during those drinking years we have always been close. Their names are Doris and Raymond, and they married a brother and sister. When we get together, which is often, for we live on the same road, there come times in the talking and card-playing, and maybe even in the light beer now and then, when we will bring up those days. Most people understand how it was. Our story isn't uncommon. But for us it helps to compare our points of view.

How else would I know, for instance, that Raymond saw me the first time I hid my father's belt? I pulled it from around his waist while he was passed out, and then I buried it in the woods. I kept doing it after that. Our father couldn't understand why his belt was always stolen when he went to town drinking. He even accused his *shkwebii* buddies of the theft. But I had good reasons. Not only was he embarrassed, afterward, to go out with his pants held up by rope, but he couldn't snake his belt out in anger and snap the hooked buckle end in the air. He couldn't hit us with it. Of course, being resourceful, he used other things. There was a board. A willow wand. And there was himself—his hands and fists and boots—and things he could throw. But eventually it became easy to evade him, and after a while we rarely suffered a bruise or a scratch. We had our own place in the woods, even a little campfire for the cold nights. And we'd take money from him every chance we got, slip it from his shoe, where he thought it well hidden. He became, for us, a thing to be avoided, outsmarted, and exploited. We survived off him as if he were a capricious and dangerous line of work. I suppose we stopped thinking of him as a human being, certainly as a father.

I got my growth earlier than some boys, and, one night when I was thirteen and Doris and Raymond and I were sitting around wishing for something besides the oatmeal and commodity canned milk I'd stashed so he couldn't sell them, I heard him coming down the road. He was shouting and making noise all the way to the house, and Doris and Raymond looked at me and headed for the back window. When they saw that I wasn't coming, they stopped. C'mon, *ondaas*, get with it—they tried to pull me along. I shook them off and told them to get out quickly—I was staying. I think I can take him now, is what I said.

He was big; he hadn't yet wasted away from the alcohol. His nose had been pushed to one side in a fight, then slammed back to the other side, so now it was straight. His teeth were half gone, and he smelled the way he had to smell, being five days drunk. When he came in the door, he paused for a moment, his eyes red and swollen, tiny slits. Then he saw that I was waiting for him, and he smiled in a bad way. My first punch surprised him. I had been practicing on a hay-stuffed bag, then on a padded board, toughening my fists, and I'd got so quick I flickered like fire. I still wasn't as strong as he was, and he had a good twenty pounds on me. Yet I'd do some damage, I was sure of it. I'd teach him not to mess with me. What I didn't foresee was how the fight itself would get right into me.

There is something terrible about fighting your father. It came on suddenly, with the second blow—a frightful kind of joy. A power surged up from the center of me, and I danced at him, light and giddy, full of a heady rightness. Here is the thing: I wanted to waste him, waste him good. I wanted to smack the living shit out of him. Kill him, if I must. A punch for Doris, a kick for Raymond. And all the while I was silent, then screaming, then silent again, in this rage of happiness that filled me with a simultaneous despair so that, I guess you could say, I stood apart from myself.

He came at me, crashed over a chair that was already broken, then threw the pieces. I grabbed one of the legs and whacked him on the ear so that his head spun and turned back to me, bloody. I watched myself striking him again and again. I knew what I was doing, but not really, not in the ordinary sense. It was as if I were standing calm, against the wall with my arms folded, pitying us both. I saw the boy, the chair leg, the man fold and fall, his hands held up in begging fashion. Then I also saw that, for a while now, the bigger man had not even bothered to fight back.

Suddenly, he was my father again. And when I knelt down next to him, I was his son. I reached for the closest rag, and picked up this piece of blanket that my father always kept with him for some reason. And as I picked it up and wiped the blood

off his face, I said to him, Your nose is crooked again. He looked
at me, steady and quizzical, as though he had never had a drink
in his life, and I wiped his face again with that frayed piece
of blanket. Well, it was a shawl, really, a kind of old-fashioned
woman's blanket-shawl. Once, maybe, it had been plaid. You
could still see lines, some red, the background a faded brown.
He watched intently as my hand brought the rag to his face.
I was pretty sure, then, that I'd clocked him too hard, that he'd
really lost it now. Gently, though, he clasped one hand around
my wrist. With the other hand he took the shawl. He crumpled
it and held it to the middle of his forehead. It was as if he were
praying, as if he were having thoughts he wanted to collect in
that piece of cloth. For a while he lay like that, and I, crouched
over, let him be, hardly breathing. Something told me to sit
there, still. And then at last he said to me, in the sober new voice
I would hear from then on, *Did you know I had a sister once?*

There was a time when the government moved everybody off
the farthest reaches of the reservation, onto roads, into towns,
into housing. It looked good at first, and then it all went sour.
Shortly afterward, it seemed that anyone who was someone
was either drunk, killed, near suicide, or had just dusted himself. None of the old sort were left, it seemed—the old kind of
people, the Gete-anishinaabeg, who are kind beyond kindness
and would do anything for others. It was during that time that
my mother died and my father hurt us, as I have said.

Now, gradually, that term of despair has lifted somewhat
and yielded up its survivors. But we still have sorrows that are
passed to us from early generations, sorrows to handle in addition to our own, and cruelties lodged where we cannot forget
them. We have the need to forget. We are always walking on
oblivion's edge.

Some get away, like my brother and sister, married now and
living quietly down the road. And me, to some degree, though

I prefer to live alone. And even my father, who recently found a woman. Once, when he brought up the old days, and we went over the story again, I told him at last the two things I had been thinking.

First, I told him that keeping his sister's shawl was wrong, because we never keep the clothing of the dead. Now's the time to burn it, I said. Send it off to cloak her spirit. And he agreed.

The other thing I said to him was in the form of a question. Have you ever considered, I asked him, given how tenderhearted your sister was, and how brave, that she looked at the whole situation? She saw that the wolves were only hungry. She knew that their need was only need. She knew that you were back there, alone in the snow. She understood that the baby she loved would not live without a mother, and that only the uncle knew the way. She saw clearly that one person on the wagon had to be offered up, or they all would die. And in that moment of knowledge, don't you think, being who she was, of the old sort of Anishinaabeg, who thinks of the good of the people first, she jumped, my father, *n'dede,* brother to that little girl? Don't you think she lifted her shawl and flew?

Lorena Fuerta ◉ Mescalero Apache/Yaqui

Anna Ghostdancer

something about knowing women
brought your hands to light and
reattached them,
reburied you with ceremony
that knowledge
brought forth tears.
I envision
hands that loved and worked and held
your sleeping children
and
I wonder
did the killers understand
what they were saying
in relation to
our women
in their world?
They must have been afraid of you
to mutilate you so,
to try to keep your hands
from being raised against them
now
yet it is your hands I see
reaching out
with a warning to us all:
something in the murder of a woman isolated
from her people
reminds us
there are worse ways of dying
than in fighting for our freedom

Revah Mariah S. Gover ⓢ Skidi/Tohono O'odham

Conjure

There is a story.
There is a story that is painted upon the walls of flesh and skin,
Rises before the eyes in splashes of red ocher and cold clear wind.

The storyteller stretches the mind.
Leaping agile memory disguised as song.
It is all there trapped, or liberated, by coffee-stained words
    woven
Into the warm breath of cigarette smoke and desperate
    remembrance.
I saw it once—it shimmered and fell heavily against my auntie's
    memory of Uppitt.
Uppitt. I smell it on the crisp taste of wind fingering my hair,
    watering my eyes.

They say that the story doesn't change, only the storyteller.
Maybe the feelings are all the same—but a baby dying from
    hunger knows
That it is loved as his mother, and hers, conjure milk from
    barren breasts.

There is no miracle of imagined milk for those starving
    for the purity of Truth.
She sheaths herself in chameleon red and doesn't want to be
    recognized anymore.
Orphans, alienated from wardance songs, these babies
    are as husks.
Crouch in alleyways, huddle in dirty jackets, suckle booze,
    smell of piss and cedar.

Beauty can be found in the mouth of the teller.
The story creates the world. The Word. There is a story.
There is a story that is painted upon the walls of flesh and skin.
The brush of certainty caresses it sweetly with earth and tears.
There is a story with a different ending, imagining birth.

◉ ◉ ◉

Long Division

I reside in a world of halves. Half desert, half plain—
a dimension where lightning cracks a watercolor sky;
sometimes violet, sometimes gray—jagged mountains
mirroring infinite black and infused points of light.

A world in halves, a world in halves; my Uppitt knew.
He believed in educated power, the need for alien thoughts
spun into alien words, the birth of this new world and our
survival this way. Eyes closed and dreaming, secrets
burrowed a thorny chasm of hope.

I am Mother, today, I am Woman. A tornado of warring
sentiments—born of the soul, etched in the womb, desire
within desire—and how do I keep either side from winning?

Today, I struggle to find my way in death, or rebirth—
unable to conjure myself in breath or sound. My spirit
crumbles with the living and turned out of my body
I don't have the strength to navigate the Stars. What I
lost Uppitt always had—I see him sometimes, pointing
to his Mother, the Moon.

Singing lullabies my tongue twists around the shape-sounds,
and colored hues of an enemy language. Clear tones of alabaster
wince at the brown of my eyes, the black of my son's hair,
the pulse of my Heluska heart and his rhythmic sleep-breath.

I reside in a world of halves. Wielding arrows and obsidian
knives I bare resistance to those who would suck my being
through the nipple of Manifest Destiny—masquerading
as Christ, ordained as God. Shuddering, I am horrified
by good intentions and smallpox.

Wrapped in a blanket of fear I clutch diplomas to ward off
evil. Refuse to dream, turn my face away from grace—
strive to embrace and deny who I am, who my children are,
and who we will always be.

I have given birth and I have created with words.
I have danced and I have sung the old songs.
Clutching the earth by my fingernails I will

invent a song that will save me as I walk this ledge.
A blade of sweetgrass between my teeth, I pray.
Words you cannot hear, and I cannot say.

Linda LeGarde Grover ◉ Ojibwe

Chi-Ko-ko-koho and the Boarding School Prefect

From my owl's nest home, unsteady greasy oak
covered by cowhide long oblivious
to claws tough and curving as old tree roots
I breathe the night breeze, starry broken glass.

I am Chi-Ko-ko-koho. My black-centered
unblinking owl eyes see past the dark
growl of this old bear den of a bar,
through stinging fog of unintended
blasphemy, tobacco's tarry prayers
stuck and dusty on a hammered tin ceiling,
to grieving spirits mirrored by my own.
I am Chi-Ko-ko-koho, young among owls
as young among lush crimson blooms of death
is the embryonic seedling in my chest,
the rooting zygote corkscrew in my chest,
these days all but unseen, a pink seaspray
sunset on a thick white coffee cup.
My grieving spirit hardly notices
though, in this old bear den of a bar.

My owl head turns clear round when I see him.
I am Chi-Ko-ko-koho, I blink away
smoke and fog, my head swivels back
and he's still there, the prefect. He's still there
and real, not some ghost back to grab my throat
again with those heavy old no-hands of his
or crack my brother's homesick skinny bones
on cold concrete tattooed by miseries
of other Indian boys who crossed his path.

To the darkness of this bear den of a bar
he's brought his own sad spirit for a drink.

I am Chi-Ko-ko-koho, but who he sees
is Kwiiwizens, a boy bent and kneeling
beneath the prefect's doubled leather strap,
and Kwiiwizens I am. My belly feels
a tiny worm the color of the moon
writhe in laughter at my cowardice
as that now embodied ghost, the old prefect
step-drags, step-drags his dampened moccasins
to my end of the bar. The flowers weep
above his toes in mourning for us all.

He asks me for a nickel for a beer.
With closed eyes Kwiiwizens waits for the strap.

Chi-Ko-ko-koho dives from his grimy perch
to yank the apparition by the hair,
then flies him past the blind face of the moon
to drop him in the alley back behind
the dark growl of this old bear den of a bar.

Indizhinikaaz Kwiiwizens,
gaye indizhinikaaz Chi-Ko-ko-koho.
Ni maajaa. Mi-iw. I leave him there.

I am Chi-Ko-ko-koho. I leave him there
under stars of broken glass. I leave him there.

Debra Haaland   ⊚   Laguna Pueblo

Mother's Love

I would take her back if I could. She used to be strong, and she used her weight to get her way with my dad so many times. With us too. But now I try not to remember that too much. As I see her lying here, small and helpless, I wish we could go back. I'd probably be more understanding.

My shift is the swing plus graveyard. My sisters-in-law and nieces come during the day and once in a while in the evening to give me time off, but I don't mind if they never give me time off. I'd move into this hospital if I could. I love my mother. The only complaint I have is that the nurses wake us up in the middle of the night to take blood samples and her temperature. But I guess it's a good time for me to rearrange her pillows and give her a sip of water. They all say what a good patient she is. I have to agree. She has more patience with the staff here than she ever had with us. But right now it's easy to remember more of the good things about her.

My mother was tall for a Pueblo woman—before she began to shrink under the weight of her years. We can now probably see eye-to-eye. She always dressed in loose cotton dresses which she kept covered with full bib aprons. Her clothes were never dirty until her eyesight began to fail. Her black leather lace-up shoes looked new for years; in fact I thought they were new for the longest time. When canvas shoes came out, she thought them more comfortable but harder to keep clean.

I was an eager student when she decided to teach me to sew and cross stitch. She taught me how to skin a deer and how to slice the meat paper thin for jerky. "Never use a dull knife," she'd say with great expression in her voice. What a chore it was to hang the meat up when it was wet. I had to use a stepladder to reach the lines my dad strung from our boxcar home to the light post. And for the first several days the meat was so heavy. We had to take it down every night and put it up every morning before I went to school.

When it finally dried, we were careful to use only what we needed, making it last as long as we could. The wonderful sweet smell of deer meat cooking in a pot with rice or hominy made my mouth water, and I felt all my hard work was worth it.

I was the only girl in my family, so I had to learn all the things about Laguna domestic life by myself. My two brothers had to find women whose mothers taught them as much as my mother taught me. They have many good points, but being here with mom right now isn't one of them.

My mother also taught me how to cook. That was the best thing I learned from her. There was no end to her love of being in the kitchen. I too grew up preferring the kitchen to any other room in the house. She never liked me getting in her way when she was busy but she'd assign me tasks that I could do out of her way.

One task was to chop very small pieces of wood to use for making piki. She had a beautiful flat stone that had turned glossy black like the obsidian arrowhead my dad kept in his top drawer. The stone was placed above a fire pit in a little piki house he built for her out in back. She wasn't the only one to use it; the other women used it too, but I only had to chop the small pieces of wood for her. She was an expert at making piki. She'd spread the corn batter so thin on the hot stone without ever making a face. I don't think she ever had one blister on her hand as a result of it.

After mom rolled the piki bread up, it was my job to put each one in the special cardboard box she kept them in. I put sheets of newspaper between each layer. When she was done, I cleaned out the ashes from underneath the stone and spread ground unshelled sunflower seeds on top to keep the stone well seasoned. We ate the piki only on special occasions. On regular days we ate oven bread with every meal.

My mom also let me take the basket of hominy outside to rinse under the spigot that was in the middle of the camp. That was something I could do by myself. My mom had a large shallow yucca basket, which I rinsed and rinsed the hominy in. Once a year we always got white corn from my auntie and uncle at Jemez Pueblo. We would go to the feast day on November 12th, which was right after harvest. My dad usually traded my uncle for moccasins that he had made. Uncle and auntie had seven children, and they always needed shoes for them.

Sometimes the corn was still moist when we got it home, so mom would lay it on a white sheet on top of our house until it dried. I'd help her grind some of it into corn meal and the rest she made into hominy by boiling the loose kernels with ashes. By rinsing them afterward, the outside shell came off and then mom dried them again. I loved the smell of hominy simmering on a hot stove. It steamed up the windows and I could even smell it from outside. My mom's cooking was so dear to me. When I met Ray, the man who was to be my husband, at NAU in Flagstaff, I realized that I loved him when he made me feel the way my mom's cooking did.

My mother never *just* cooked. The food I ate while growing up was nourishing for my body and my spirit. When we all sat down for a meal, my dad would pray in Laguna and invite the spirits inside to eat with us. As we ate, my mother and father would give us advice about listening to our teachers and how to treat the people we shared this world with. They would tell us how we came by the food—someone had grown it, an animal had given its life to us so we could live, my dad had worked hard to buy us the food we needed. As we ate, the important words of my parents went in us, nourishing our hearts and minds, like, I imagined, the gospel nourished the Bible people on the street corners in downtown Winslow.

Winslow was my home from the time I was born until I moved out at age eighteen. My dad had moved there from Jemez when he was twenty. My mom went to Winslow from Laguna. She first helped her older sister with her four children, then she married my dad. They had originally met at St. Catherine's boarding school.

Even though we lived in the old boxcars, ours was like a real house. My dad put sandbags all around the bottom, making the metal box appear like it had a foundation on the sandy ground. My mother sewed curtains and decorated the walls with Navajo rugs and baskets she had acquired throughout the years. Our home was uncluttered, displaying only items that were useful in some way. Considering all the other boxcars in the camp, ours stood out for the care my parents gave it. Nothing was ever out of place inside or out.

As I say, my mom was hard to get along with sometimes, but my dad loved her. Once when I was older and my parents had moved away from the Indian camp to the Desert Gardens subdivision, I drove up to see my dad brushing his teeth and washing his face outside. He told me my mom had cleaned the bathroom and she wouldn't let him use it! He thought it was funny. I was angry. Sometimes it seemed that only her feelings mattered.

As I see her now, she would comply with anything. She'd probably let the little ones jump on the beds and put their feet on her furniture. In fact, she probably wouldn't notice. When I was young, it was almost a sin to even sit on the beds once they were made. My mother taught us discipline, and with that discipline came an appreciation of all the things my mom and dad worked for.

◉

My dad used to speak Laguna, Jemez, and English fluently, and he could get by in Spanish, Navajo, and Hopi. He was brilliant. He made friends wherever he went working on the railroad, and he always told them to stop in to see us. My mom cooked for them too.

Some Navajo people dad knew would often stop at the Indian camp on their way from here to there, in their horse-drawn wagon. It was already in the 1940s and they still used an old brown and white nag who was seemingly too old to pull their creaking heap of wood. My dad called the woman Nanabah. Nanabah was very big and she was never without large turquoise and silver bracelets and a squash blossom necklace that rested high on her enormous bosom. It stood out against the solid velvet shirts she wore. Her hair was always pulled back in a chongo with a woven wool hair wrap. My dad said her husband was a jeweler and a sheepherder.

Nanabah would climb slowly down from the wagon, her full, brightly-colored cotton print skirt swaying steadily over her large frame as she walked. She'd knock on the door of our house while her husband sat in the wagon, his hands holding the reins tight, as if the grandma horse would run away with him. My mom would open the door smiling and the woman would say, "Hastiin hungry!" Every time, throughout the years, she'd always say, "Hastiin hungry!" So my mom would wave him inside too, and I would lead the horse to the cottonwood tree in the back of our house. Whenever I'd see them coming through the gate, I'd tell my mom, "Here comes Hastiin Hungry." I thought Hungry was his last name. My dad would carry on the conversation as best he could, while we all sat there smiling. They liked my mom's green chile meat and potato stew the best. Whenever they left, they took bread and other food for their journey.

After eating, Hastiin and Nanabah always brought in mutton for my mom and she was always grateful. I especially loved the ribs. I'd immediately hang the ribs on a bent coat hanger attached to the tree, and after the ribs dried mom roasted them for a long time until the meat was very crisp and all the grease was in the bottom of the pan. The ribs would take on the rich smoky flavor of the cedar wood from the oven. The grease dripped through our fingers as we ate them, and I loved dipping my bread in the warm sheep grease afterwards. It was good for my hair and skin, my dad would tell me. We thought of our Navajo friends while eating the mutton, and I could see that my mom was happy for the exchange of food.

❀

About every hour or so, I have to exercise my mother's legs. She has only walked a few times in the last week. She gets too tired. She is so thin she doesn't have much energy. So I raise her legs up and down. I pull gently on her arms to stretch them. She eats a little bit, but lately it has been difficult for her to keep anything down. The doctor will x-ray her tomorrow to see inside. She still likes her coffee, with cream and sugar, but now she can only drink a few sips and no more.

❀

She had always had such a good appetite, although she would never eat anyone else's food but her own. When we had community dinners, she'd take a pot of red chile stew and three or four loaves of bread and that was all she would eat. While everyone else, including myself, had plates filled with Jell-O salads, potato salads, meat loaf, and cake, mom offered no explanations for only a single bowl of *her* stew and two slices of bread in front of her.

Whenever someone in the camp had a deer dinner, the whole camp was expected to partake. My mother never went, but she'd send me instead. I could never say no. I would cringe in front of a bowl of deer stew that had turned black because the hunter's wife did not wash the blood out of her meat. Once I walked into a home where the family had used their washtub for a pot. The stew bubbled and boiled, and although it had to be the cleanest stew in Winslow, the flavor of borax and soap was sure death for my taste buds. I'd rush home to eat straight hot green chile to kill the awful taste in my mouth. I'd tell the stories of what I had seen and tasted, and my mom always had answers for why the food was poor. My dad would laugh, while my mom shook her head in disappointment.

☙

It's Tuesday, March 23rd at about 8 PM. My mother has lain in this hospital bed for a month now. My sister-in-law came at 6 PM so I could go down to the cafeteria and get dinner. The cooks don't know any better. I ate a hamburger that was cooked on a dirty grill. The taste of carbon was heavy, and the bun was greasy on the top. It sat, without meaning, on a black plastic plate with wilted lettuce. I could've gone home to cook something good for me, but I was afraid part of me wouldn't want to return. My husband misses me.

Ray and I haven't really talked since mom has been here. He'll come by soon to kiss me goodnight, but he doesn't like hospitals, says they smell like disinfectant and pureed beef. Although I am immune to the smells, I understand. He works for the Forest Service and is used to the outdoors. He wants to die at the hands of a bear or mountain lion, not in a hospital. I hope he does. He would be miserable here.

☙

My mother woke up for a while this evening when Ray came in. She smiled. He stood by her bed and rubbed the arm with no tubes coming out of it; it's healing from the skin getting torn off with a bandage. The nurse that day was new and apparently hadn't cared for old people. She should've asked me. I know all there is to know about my mother. Ray kissed us both and left. He's going down to the Gila Mountains early in the morning.

Like many other nights, I sit and read, or work on the *New York Times* crossword puzzle book my friend Julie gave me last year. I knew I'd eventually have time. When I get tired of sitting, I walk up and down the halls, listen to the loneliness. In some rooms the only sound is the steady electronic mechanism dispensing the drip of the IV. Sugar water, antibiotics, pain killers—the patient's new family. No wonder the man in 521 ripped his out and tried to run. He didn't get far before he collapsed. There are a lot of people in here with no one. Everyone on the floor looks to be over sixty-five. The nurses often compliment me on the care I give my mother, but I don't do it for that. I do it because my mother taught me well. Besides, I want to be near if she decides to pull out of her slump. I would even welcome a mean look in her eyes.

Until two weeks ago, I was optimistic, then she began to reject food. She can eat a little, but the doctor said if she doesn't eat more she will have to put a tube in mom's stomach. Another tube, another liquid entering my mother's body. I question my decision to give the doctor the go-ahead. Just months ago she was eating fresh roasted corn and beef tamales with red chile that she had made. If I'd asked her then, "Mom, would you ever want to be fed milky baby food through a tube in your stomach if you began rejecting food?" she would have laughed and told me I already know the answer to that question.

I sit in the dark with the television on mute. David Letterman is the same no matter what night. Same show, different day. Mom wakes up for a second, snapping at me to turn off the TV. She must not realize that she no longer needs to scold me, but I turn it off anyway. I still respect her.

I sit quietly in the dark. Blinking back the thoughts that I want so badly to bury. I pray to myself. I pray that mom will get well and that I can take her home. I pray that she is free of pain. I pray to take back the words I had spoken so many years ago. In some way I feel I am partially to blame for her condition, yet

I know the limitations of my human power. We all wish, sometimes, that our parents will die. Don't we? But we never really mean it.

❂

I remember the first time I felt my words had any power over her, although as I grew older, I realized it was pure coincidence. She was yelling at me, as she often did. I prayed to myself, right then, for her to stop, no matter what. She began coughing and coughing. I stood silent and still. I did not move to pat her back or get her a glass of water. When she stopped coughing, her voice was a whisper! I was so happy inside, although I did not show it. I was free from her over-burdening voice for a week! I thought she'd see it as God giving her a chance to change, but she fell right back into her ways. And again I dreaded it. Even when she talked calmly to me, her loud voice was all I heard and even though she was sometimes nice, it was the meanness that I remembered back then.

My hair was long, thick, and beautiful, but my mother never saw it so much as a gift as something to grab me by. I wished so many times that I was bald, and when I finally decided to chop it off, I almost went into shock. All my friends laughed at me, saying that my mother wasn't that bad. My dad hugged me and said I still looked pretty. I cut it up to my neck, and it aroused no change in mom.

It was after I cut my hair that I went to a dance at Laguna village with my cousins. Back then, four or five Spanish guys from Seboyeta, the little Spanish land grant north of Laguna, would come down to play for the night of the feast. We always went home for the feast day on September 19th. The dance was always held at the Smokehouse, the old meeting hall in the center of the village. Now the building stands empty, but it used to blare Spanish rancheras and Hank Williams on feast nights. Someone said they called it the Smokehouse because it had a little cast iron stove that smoked incessantly when wood burned inside. No matter what the men did to try to fix it, it still smoked. The noise of the band, with teenagers and old people alike two-stepping and swinging, drowned out the sound of the creaking pine floors.

My dad said I could go, and so my cousins and I rode the five miles from Mesita to Laguna in the back of my uncle's blue Ford pick-up. He was supposed to pick us up at 10:30.

About 8:30, after my mom was finished replastering the mud ovens near my grandma's house, she told my dad to take her where I was. And as always, he could not say no. He waited in the truck as she barreled into the Smokehouse, where I was engaged in a waltz with a handsome cowboy from Paguate village. I had never before had so much fun! Unfortunately my back was to mother at the time. My partner didn't know it was my mother, otherwise he would have warned me. She was covered in dried mud, her jet hair drawn back in a faded red bandanna.

I was devastated when my head jerked back like a whiplash victim's. My good time ended in great embarrassment. The band was so surprised that they momentarily stopped playing when I was dragged out to my dad's waiting truck. On the way back to my grandma's I sat with Smokey in the back of the truck, his warm furry body across my lap catching my confusion of hurtful and angry tears.

It was before I cut my hair, though, that I made the mistake of poking my head in the truck window as mom was leaving for town. I really wanted to go. I had saved up ten dollars from helping my uncle in his fields during two weeks I had spent in Mesita, and I wanted to buy a record player. She grabbed me by the hair and started driving. I ran for awhile until my legs fell under me and until she got tired of holding on. We were almost to the end of the dirt road that led to the camp from the highway.

My mother was the only woman in camp who had ever learned to drive. By then I was almost a teenager and all I thought of was the day I would leave.

◈

My dad was sad when I told him I was going to join the Navy. My brothers had, so why shouldn't I? I don't think he wanted to be left alone. My mother never physically hurt him, but she often displayed displeasure in her life. He felt partially responsible, which is why he worked so hard to please her. After all, he thought, she would never have gone to Winslow were it not for him. Perhaps if she had not gone to Winslow, her life would have turned out the way she wanted it to, and she would not have been so angry. Now it is difficult for me to know what kind of life she would have wanted, but when she was younger I just knew I wasn't in her original plan.

My parents moved back to Mesita, after dad retired, into a little rock house my grandpa had built for my mom. It was only a shell, and my dad put on a roof, built wood floors, installed wooden-framed windows and cooking and heating stoves. When the village got electricity in 1970, he wired the house himself. He never lived to see indoor plumbing. When he died in his corn field in 1972 my mom cried so hard. For the first time, I realized that my mother was able to show her feelings of love, and I had wished it was my body she was crying over.

◈

The doctors said there is nothing more they can do for her, short of putting the tube in her stomach, so I am taking my mother home to her house in Mesita. She deserves to die with family all around. Ray and my brothers are there. My sisters-in-law are cleaning the house and preparing my mother's bed.

◈

I ride in the ambulance with no lights, no sound or display. The red and white van glides down the highway, going the speed limit, as I look out the window at the familiar landscape under a warm and windy sky. I truly appreciate the red mesas, the purple outline of Mt. Taylor in the distance, the endless sea of dried grass and the tiny skeletons of prairie dogs and rattlers. The No. 19 windmill still turns after God knows how many years.

I look at my mother, her closed eyes magnified by thick black-framed glasses. I stroke her thinned gray hair against paper-like skin, wishing, at this moment, that I had had children. I have no one to pass on the wealth of knowledge she has shared with me over these fifty years.

As we exit at the 117, she opens her eyes, seemingly feeling the large red mesa reflecting a certain glow of light from the sun which it faces. She sighs, squeezes my hand as tight as her bony weightless hand will allow, and she smiles.

☉

That look of peace accompanied her as she faded from us that very day. In her honor I cooked all the things she loved. At the funeral feast, many people had good stories to tell about my mother, and as I ate, their words filled me.

Inés Hernández-Avila ☺ Nimipu/Tejana

Tough Audience

Indi'n women are tough
we can see through things,
people, situations, games,
and cut to the heart of it all

There's an assessment that goes on
without the need for words
It happens in a flash
Suddenly it all becomes clear
sometimes too clear
if you know what I mean

And the response?

It might be a look right at you
It might be a look intentionally
away from you
It might be a look down
It might be a look up

Pay attention to the look
Read it
Get it
Be right there with the look
It's called being in sync
with the cosmos

☺ ☺ ☺

Brother's Passing

for "Cy" Narcisse Bierle

In the longhouse our brothers
dance to the spirit-calling songs of the *walah'tsa*
the Seven Drums
offering themselves for you
with loving devoted intent
marking the place where your body rests
on this sacred earthen floor
making sure the exact spot is known

we follow the lead of the wise ones
guiding us through the night
attentive to the renewal of our people
as we send you home

the sky world opens
as the path is sung into creation for you
such richness of voice
of heart united
of communal vision
of joyous eternity
there is brilliance everywhere
as the story of your life
is told
here is when hearts share
how you touched them
this is your honoring song

singing I see the spirit ones appear
to bring your noble warrior spirit over
the voices of the Seven Drums

call them
call them
call them
call them
sing them into the lines of flowers
reaching from your resting body to the stars
our brothers dancing help you rise to meet them

With the dancing and the singing and the prayer
with the dancing and the singing and the prayer
You begin the walk to the place of peace
the oldest ones come from the oldest times
the ones who knew you in your life
are the first in the lines
to receive you
hands outstretched
Your journey is protected
Your spirit steps are blessed in beauty
as our spirits join to help you
with the dancing and the singing and the prayer
with the dancing and the singing and the prayer

singing I feel your love strong heart
and your truth is everywhere
beloved grandson
beloved son
beloved brother
beloved father
beloved warrior
singing I am alert to the wonder
and the whole earth dances for you

Linda Noel ✆ Konkow Maidu

Close to Bone

There are few secrets strung between us, but
Dust of broken-hearted memories echo off scarred

Bone walls. A dark woman's shadow on every beat
Of cloud-strung skies and storms passed. No, you

And I were never stitched star to star, or did the hot
Dance of thunder on ice or even been star-struck

Simultaneously. But thread spun of gut still breathes
You out of me, holds the remaining cracked cobalt

Blue beads worn around the neck of me and you.
They rattle the length of my backbone when I hear

That gentle guitar skimming all these summers
And re-threading the weathered bead secrets. Some

Are chipped shells we dug from some muddy beach,
Others are smooth driftwood fallen far upriver

Out of the mouth of winter, and some are small, small
Stones hanging close enough to clang on bone.

Laura Tohe ⊙ Navajo

In Dinétah

On this historic occasion 130 years after the signing of the peace treaty of 1868.
Within Dinétah the People's Spirit Remains Strong 1998. These words are for
my people, the Diné, who endured colossal hardship and near-death and continue
to endure.

In the people's memory are the stories
This we remember:

I
Ałkidą́ą́' adajiní nít'ę́ę̀,
They say long time ago in time immemorial:
the stories say we emerged from
the umbilical center of this sacred earth into
    the Glittering World
smoothed by Twin Heroes,
sons of White Shell Woman,
who journeyed to find their father
and aided by Spider Woman who taught them
how not to fear the perilous journey.
They say the sun, father to the Twin Heroes,
gave them the knowledge to slay the monsters
so that the world would be safe.

We lived according to the teachings of the Holy People
to dwell within the sacred mountains:
Sis Naajiní rising to the east,
Tsoodził rising to the south,
Dook'o'osłííd rising to the west,
Dibé Nítsaa rising to the north
We raised our families,
planted our corn,
greeted the dawn with our prayers,
and followed the path of corn pollen

Every day was a new beginning
. . . in Beauty
. . . in Beauty.

II
The ancestors predicted it would happen,
that the wind would shift and bring
light-colored men from across the big water
who would shatter our world.
They would arrive wearing metal coats
riding strange beautiful animals,
would arrive in clothes that brushed the earth
carrying crossed sticks to plunge into Dinétah.
In their zealous urge they sought cities of gold.
Later we learned they came to take
our land, our lives, our spirits.

Did they not know we are
all created from the same elements?
Rainclouds for hair,
fingernails formed from beautiful seashells,
the rivers flow through our veins, our lifeline,
from wind we came to life,
with thunder voices we speak.
We fought back to protect ourselves
as we had fought with other enemies.

The world changed when
the light-colored men brought their women.
It was then we knew they meant to stay.
They invented ways to justify what they wanted,
Manifest Destiny, assimilation, colonization.
And, most of all, they wanted the land.
One day a man wearing red clothes appeared.

Bi'éé' Łichii'í, Kit Carson, sent by Wáashindoon.
He brought many soldiers.
They spoke with thunder sticks
that tore into everything that we loved
to burn our beautiful peach orchards,
to slaughter our sheep in front of us,
to starve us out from Dinétah,
to do unspeakable things to us,
to wrench us from our land.
What strange fruit is this that dangles
        from the trees?
We feared for our lives
and hid among the rocks and shadows
gathering food and water when we could.

III
What was our crime?
We wanted only to live as we had
within our sacred mountains
seeking harmony, seeking long life
. . . in Beauty
. . . in Beauty.

Others had their death march:
The Trail of Tears, Auschwitz,
The Door of No Return in the House of Slaves.
We are Diné.
We too had our death march forced on us.
When The Long Walk began, we witnessed our women
        murdered and raped
our children and relatives swept away in the rushing currents
        of the Rio Grande

We heard explosions that silenced mothers giving birth
    behind the rocks.
We saw the newborn and the elderly left behind.
We saw our warriors unable to defend us.
And even now the land we crossed still holds
        the memory of our people's tears, cries, and blood.
Kit Carson marched us three hundred miles away.
In the distance we saw our sacred mountains
        becoming smaller and smaller.
We were torn from the land that held our birth stems.
We were taken to the land that was not us.
We were taken to the desolate place without trees or vegetation.
Where the men picked out undigested corn from animal dung
    to eat.
Where young women were raped.
We called this place Hweełdi,
this place of starvation,
this place of near-death
this place of extreme hardship.

IV
We returned to our land after four years.
Our spirits ragged and weary.
And vowed that we would never be separated from Dinétah;
        the earth is our strength
We have grown strong.
We are the children of White Shell Woman.
We are the people of the original clans she created.
We are female warriors and male warriors—
    Manuelito, Barboncito
We are the Code Talkers who used our language to help
    save America.
We are Annie Wauneka who taught us to have faith
    in the white man's medicine.

We are the sons and daughters of activists and other
    unsung heroes
        "when Indian men were the finest men there were."
We are the hands that create fine turquoise and silver jewelry.
We are the women who resisted relocation
    when the government came with papers and fences.
We are teachers, cowboys, lawyers, musicians.
We are medicine people, doctors, nurses, college professors.
We are artists, soldiers, politicians, architects, farmers.
We are sheep herders, engineers, singers, comediennes.
We are weavers of baskets and exquisite blankets.
We are bus drivers, welders, ranchers, dishwashers.
We are the people who offer prayers during the cycles of the day.
We are Diné.
In Beauty it was begun.
In Beauty it continues.
    In Beauty,

        In Beauty,

            In Beauty,

                In Beauty.

Karenne Wood ◎ Monacan

In Memory of Shame
for Joy Harjo

Remember, before we were born
that we swam a blood river.
Curled in women's songs
we pushed toward our lives
because we wanted to breathe air.
We were not guilty of anything then.

It took us years to learn every
layer, to unwrap delicately
like a lover, our shame
to find after all that we were the ones
who pressed it into our flesh
who loved it and
gave it the shapes of ourselves

because it was our fault and because we did nothing wrong
because we spoke and because we had nothing to say
because we were ignorant and because we knew too much
because we neglected our children and because we wanted
    to protect them
because we drank and because we stopped drinking
because we were industrious and because we had no energy
because we were young, old, fat, bony, spineless, cocky,
    selfish, selfless, frigid, immoral, guilty

    because we loved too much or not enough
    because we couldn't fry an egg correctly
    because the house hid dust in its corners
    because we stayed and because we left
    because our faces were the wrong ones

because we were treated disrespectfully
because we were children or women or not
white or just not enough.

Remember, we let our shame go.
After all the time in the world.
We watched it scuttle toward cracks in our lives
like a prehistoric crab yanked from its shell—
almost formless, almost afraid, but wide-eyed
it peered back at us
and we knew it as our own
so much a part of us
we hardly know which of us is hiding.

3 New Age Pocahontas

This section explores the popular image of Native American women as we write into and against stereotype. When I first began work on the anthology, I talked with Jim Cihlar about what I wanted the book to do. We spoke of our hope that the anthology would question and challenge popular images of Native American women. Too often Native Americans in general are portrayed as tragic victims or, equally harmful, as emblems of the New Age or pseudo-spiritual ideal. You might imagine here the warrior at the "End of the Trail," or the mystical shaman selling sweats to tourists. No matter what you picture, it is unlikely that even those stereotypes evoke an image of a woman. Much has been said about the invisibility of American Indian women. As a teacher of Native American literature, I often ask my students what they see when I say the word *Indian*. With rare exceptions, what they report is a male figure. When asked to report images of Native women they recall Pocahontas, Sacajawea, or they present an image of the ubiquitous Indian Princess. Sometimes, still, the degraded "squaw" is the first thing that comes to mind. When I ask students to name a living Indian woman they can sometimes get to Cherokee leader Wilma Mankiller, though they do not know what it is she does. More recently, Winona LaDuke has made the presence of Native American woman real in the public perception. It would be great if the stereotype we had to live up to were of "No Nukes" LaDuke, but in reality, we have a long way to go before any image matches up with the truth of who Native American women are today.

The poems and prose contained in this section react to popular images with humor and serious attention. What does it mean to Native American women to be told by a stranger (and told often, trust me) that "my great-great grandmother was an Indian Princess?" Annie Cecilia Smith considers just that question in her humorous essay. Susan Deer Cloud tells us what "Her Pocahontas" meant to her in a poem on dolls. In the title for this section, we revised that historical figure's name to "New Age Pocahontas" in order to convey the popularly accepted notion of a woman whose reality is obscured by a myth adopted into the American consciousness. As a "New Age" Pocahontas, she is also that mystical great-great grandmother whose shared heritage is supposed to bring us all together, even while she serves to distance us. Lise Erdrich's "Fleur-de-Lis" tells, through the life of an Indian woman who lived long ago, how a young woman in the present is led by ancient connection to a crucial moment when she might recognize the power inherent in traditional women's art.

Here too are poems that deal with body image, with kinship even through divisions along skin color within Native communities, and poems like those by Linda LeGarde Grover and Marcie Rendon that confront spirituality for sale in the name of Native Americans. Similarly, the story "Miracle" by Terry Gomez shows how spiritual movements can spread across tribes and territories to bring nations together. Finally, this section

ends with Venaya Yazzie's poem "after powwow," that says
it all for me in its images of real pow-wow princesses—Indian
women who are sweaty and tired and hungry—all hanging
together in friendship as the night breaks to dawn.

The work in this section is terribly important to me. I live
in a region where many folks wake up to the Land O'Lakes butter maiden on their breakfast table each morning. My job is
clear: to present writing that reveals the complexity of Native
American communities, that examines women's roles and shows
Native Americans as dynamic, vibrant, and most importantly,
present—present in the world we all share.

Heid E. Erdrich

Susan Deer Cloud ¤ Mohawk/Blackfeet

Her Pocahontas

> *"Why will you take by force*
> *what you may have quietly by love?"*
> Powhatan, father of Pocahontas

Her Pocahontas was a doll given to her by her mother.
Her Pocahontas was an earth-skinned, dark-haired,
    amber-eyed baby
pressed into her three-year-old arms starting to reach
    past infancy
and innocence. "This doll's name is Pocahontas," her mother said.
"This doll is Indian like me. This doll is Indian like you.
Take good care of her. Hold her close to your heart."

Her Pocahontas was the most her mother ever said about
    being Indian.
It was the 1950s. People had secrets. People kept silent.
No one talked about it, and the children didn't know why.
Her Pocahontas was a soft, sad darkness who couldn't cry,
whose eyes never closed, who had an invisible tongue.
Her Pocahontas liked to be sung to deep in the forest.

Her Pocahontas was nothing like the dolls the other girls had.
Their dolls were Christmas presents with blue eyes,
    curly blonde hair,
petite plastic noses. Their dolls would never need nose jobs
    or smell
fear. Their dolls had eyes that shut so they wouldn't have to take
everything in. Their dolls cried fake tears. They made an awful
whining sound if you turned them upside-down.

Her Pocahontas was Indian. The other girls played house
    with dolls
that had skin like refined sugar for baking cakes. They expected

their dolls to grow up, to be like the actresses they worshipped
on vast movie screens—blonde, pug-nosed Doris Day always
"holding out," golden, pout-lipped Marilyn hinting with winks
she "put out." Her Pocahontas had technicolor visions
        in the woods.

Her Pocahontas was a doll with a short life expectancy.
Her Pocahontas was a baby who knew better than to cry. No one
talked about it, but there was an unspoken memory of soldiers
and death. Her Pocahontas had a body dark as night,
        undomesticated
as stars, naked as dreams. The other girls hated her Pocahontas.
They had their own Pocahontas, a confection of lies.

Their Pocahontas had two white Johns and became white herself.
Their Pocahontas was a fantasy that popped up
        on medicine bottles,
cigar lids and butter boxes. Their Pocahontas was a film star,
        first
a squaw saving the White Man in bad cowboy-and-Indian
        movies, last
a buckskin-Barbie disguised by Disney as politically correct.
Any girl could be one. Her Pocahontas knew the truth
but couldn't speak.

When her mother died too young, her eldest brother asked her
after the funeral, "Whatever happened to that doll Ma gave you—
Pocahontas?" She stood there in the whirling snow, cradling
darkness close to her heart, and couldn't remember.
"Maybe," she told him, "she died of smallpox, of arms and legs
broken for trying to bring back the old dances, of a tongue
slit for speaking her own language."

Her Pocahontas was a doll given to her by her dead mother.

Heid E. Erdrich ⊠ Ojibwe

Butter Maiden and Maize Girl Survive Death Leap

Even now, Native American Barbie gets only so many roles:
Indian Princess, Pocahontas, or, in these parts, Winona—
maiden who leapt for brave love from the rock
that overlooks that river town where eagles mate.

In my day, she might have been asked to play
Minnehaha, laughing waters, or the lovely one
in the T.V. corn oil ads: "We call it maize . . ."
Or even Captain Hook's strangely Asian Tiger Lily.

Oh, what I would have done for a Chippewa Barbie!
My mother refused to buy tourist souvenir princesses
in brown felt dresses belted with beads, stamped Made in China.
"They're stunted," Mom would say. Her lips in that line

that meant she'd said the last word. She was right, those dolls'
legs were stubby as toddlers, though they wore sexy women's
clothes. They were brown as Hershey bars and,
     Mom pointed out,
clothed in bandanas and aprons when sold as "Southern Gals."

Most confusing was the feather that sprouted at the crown
of each doll's braided hair. "Do they grow there?"
a playmate once asked, showing me the doll her father
bought her at Mount Rushmore. I recall she gazed at my

own brown locks then stated, "Your mother was an
     Indian Princess."
My denial came in an instant. My mother had warned me:
"Tell them that our tribe didn't have any royalty."
But there was a problem of believability, you see.

Turns out Mom had floated in the town parade
in feathers, raven wig and braids, when crowned "Maiden"
to the college "Brave" in the year before she married.
Oh, Mom . . . you made it hard on us, what you did at eighteen,

and worse, the local rumor that it was *you* on the butter box
from the Land O'Lakes that graced most tables in our tiny town.
You on their toast each morning, you the object of the joke,
the trick boys learned of folding the fawn-like Butter Maiden's

naked knees up to her chest to make a pair of breasts!
I cannot count the times I argued for Mom's humble status.
How many times I insisted she was no princess, though a beauty
who just happened to have played along in woodland drag
      one day.

I wonder, did my sisters have to answer for the princess?
      Did you?
Couldn't we all have used a real doll, a round, brown, or freckled,
jeans and shawl-wearing pow-wow teen queen? A lifelike
      Native Barbie—
better yet, two who take the plunge off lover's leap in tandem
      and survive.

Lise Erdrich ¤ Ojibway

Fleur-de-Lis

Sailboats off the coast of New England, tourist season with
postcard scenery and clambakes, and a blonde young woman
wearing crisp cotton pauses in a cool dark corner of the village
museum. Her white-clad form suggests a sail in lull, or a tall
still bird that is studying the waters. Tall girl is looking into
a glass display case where hidden things are brought to light.
Absorbing the object before her and its fluorescence, this girl
appears pale as a lily and gilded.

Gold bracelets and necklace, 18K orthodontia, a sheet of
light descending from her crown: a shiny girl. And bright.
Precious metal climbs up her long sensitive fingers and carved
ivory arms in sharp elegant statements, lingering on the stem
of her throat. The white and gold girl is a medical student at
a white and ivy green college whose founding charter in 1769
promised to educate and civilize the Indian youth of the country, by which was meant young men of the native tribes.

Ninety-nine years before that: another charter issued, a preposterous scrap of paper by which the Governor and Company
of Adventurers of England Trading into Hudson Bay assumed
exclusive rights to some 3,330,000 square miles which they
named for Rupert, the cousin of King Charles II who was influ-
enced in part by two French explorers, Pierre Esprit Radisson
and his brother-in-law, Siuer de Groseillers. (England and
France warred over fur until the Treaty of Paris in 1763, though
Radishes and Gooseberry mainly remained on a side of their
own.) In the shimmering reach of Rupert's Land, by the foam-
ing gleamy sea . . . a lone Cree hunter happened into camp.

In 1611 in Hudson's camp he was given a knife, a looking-
glass, and a handful of buttons. The Cree hunter left, making
signs that he would return, and brought back two deer and two
beaver skins with which he purchased a hatchet and sundries.

He was no stranger to trade. The Hudson's Bay Company soon spawned a Scots type of halfbreed to be the workforce and foundation of a vertical hierarchy which became the greatest corporation monopoly and colonization scheme ever known. (No white ladies lived in the land of Rupert.) The French being similarly occupied, the new race or culture dubbed Métis was often associated with rival companies. As for Captain Hudson, he and his son were set adrift by mutineers to freeze in the far north wind of Rupert's Land, in the cold and clinking sea.

By 1670 the Cree had extended their trading forays as far as Montreal, as well as establishing themselves at various forts in the interior. Autonomous groups of Chippewa had become con-solidated around the Great Lakes country and the Midewewin or Grand Medicine Society religion, which had as its purpose the preservation of the knowledge of herbs and cures and the pro-longation of life. French-Canadian voyageurs were paddling the watercourses leading from Three Rivers, Quebec, and Montreal to the Great Lakes region and onward, paddling the canoes of explorers and fur trading companies, singing their rousing songs and leaving their language and their names on natural features all the way—rivers, rocks, trees, trails and children—guiding traders and establishing cordial relations with any Indians (especially the women). The following year St. Lusson formally claimed for France all of the interior of North America.

(Intense competition for the beaver trade commenced, end-ing in 1763 with the military defeat of France on the Plains of Abraham. Around 1760 the last French fort was abandoned in the *pays d'en haut,* the upper country of now Minnesota-Ontario, but in the 1870s a group of Scottish merchants living in Montreal established the North West Company, moving into the abandoned posts and becoming a constant thorn in the side of the HBC.)

By 1770 the HBC had several wintering traders among the

Cree. One trader wrote to complain of the frequent smoking, feasting, dancing, and conjuring of his hosts in the Lake Winnipeg area, but he was obligated much as a modern diplomat would be to spend time at cocktail parties (especially annoying the trader who knew the natives were only waiting for rival French-Canadian traders). When in Rome, do what the Romans do. Traders were also acculturating through such institutions as marriage à la façon du pays, in the custom of the country.

In 1869, progeny of these and other fur trade marriages declared themselves to be a new nation, rightful citizens of an already-country *Assiniboia* which the Dominion of Canada intended to ignore and dislodge by purchase of territory from the HBC. The mixed-blood nation established a provisional government and *Le Comité National des Métis de la Rivière Rouge*, the flag of which was decided to be a fleur-de-lis, the emblem of the French kings and golden symbol of medieval France. The lilies of France are said by some to derive their design from an arrowhead or spear.

That year a girl was born on December 10 and named for the flag that flew for the first time on that day, or perhaps for the order in which she was born, or maybe on some whim. In any case "La Fleur" was the seventh child of a buffalo hunter and his good wife, who kept a little potato patch farm on the bonny banks of the Red. Her baptismal name was recorded as Angeline and her Indian name sounded like "Shyoosh." Six older sisters went off to the Grey Nuns school and were promptly martyred in the smallpox. The sisters shone down nightly from the sky in Manitoba, and told their youngest sister to do right in God and their people, for she had the gift.

Angeline was French and Cree and Ojibway and a wee bit Scotch and traveled west and south with a group of hunters when they lost their country in the troubles of 1870 and 1885, known in Canada as the Halfbreed Rebellions.

Wandering down the course of the Souris River there were at least plenty of turtles and turtle eggs to eat, but the buffalo were scarcely to be found. A missionary priest met them on the prairie to say the daily Mass, baptisms, funerals. One day the caravan of Red River carts came upon Ojibway relatives; for the parents of Angeline had been born in a place called Pembina. Angeline saw her husband for the first time: a fierce-looking Catholic of the soldier society keeping order on the hunt. They were married in camp, by the priest. In the space of two years they were reservation Indians, with hundreds around them dying from starvation and disease while a relentless tide of settlers kept coming, hollering in greedy chorus for the remaining scrap of land.

There is a ghostly hornpipe wailing in the vale where Angeline's parents now are buried. And the little baby . . . in desperation she had gone to the hideous old woman called "Zwayzoo Nwayr" begging for her cures, pledging her own soul and anything she owned if only the baby would be spared. It was said that this creature had killed all the people in the woods around her with her bad medicine. Angeline held out to the frightening, feathered thing her beaded bag with its few coins.

The old woman snatched it as a crow will a shiny object, turning it over and over in her claws and cocking sideways her head with its bright black-bead eyes and harsh beak. "Ah . . . and so you, young fool, are gifted with the lily and yet you come to me . . . Do you not know who you are asking?" She fixed her searing gaze on Angeline, who fell at her feet crying and pray-ing but still pledging her whole being to the service of a witch. Then the Black Bird commanded her to rise and do her bidding.

"Child," said the old one whose voice turned soft and kind. "I cannot save your baby but if you will come here from this day on, all your children will live into adulthood and you will know old age and have many descendents on this earth." She handed the bag back to Angeline adding, "And you will learn all I that know. We are from the same line, but I will leave this world alone as I have lived, ever since my people died these many years ago. Only the mixed-bloods are left, and with their priest and with their greed they have turned upon their mothers." Then she flapped away into the trees.

A historian has noted the "peaceful army of the plow" surrounding the people on their wooded island, on their hill above the buffalo plain turned to wheat and grain. *God pity their patient waiting and appoint that it may not have been in vain.* There is nothing to live on but music, laughter, dancing, praying, religion, and potatoes. Every year for a hundred years, no money comes from the treaty. Then there is a party.

Angeline has eleven more children. Although she goes out to heal or bury as she is called, the smallpox does not touch her. Nor the consumption, nor even the influenza when it comes from World War I. She gets up at dawn, helps the children trap rabbits for a stew and muskrats for the trader. She shows them how to live from the woods and from the garden. They have a cow and pig and chickens. One by one as they reach an age, the children go away to Indian School. They shall do well in the white world and not come back, except to visit.

Angeline is the midwife, the medicine woman who carries her black bag into the bush. A son comes along to learn and to collect the roots and leaves and herbs. But at age twenty-one he goes to be a warrior and he dies in World War II. First he marries a white girl in the state of Washington and now it is her grandchild, only son of a seventh son, who Angeline hopes will be the doctor when he is done with school.

There is no one to show him his great gift and listen for the call. Mistakenly, he becomes an electronics engineer and millionaire. He hears one day that his grandmother has died somewhere in North Dakota, but he has never seen her. He's been

told he is part French-Canadian and that's why he is "swarthy."
The ocean waves lap his sons and daughters and their little
towheads shine. It is a land of great opportunity, he can afford a
trophy wife and a bunch of kids who he will build sand castles
with and send to an Ivy League college.

Angeline rode her buggy to Mass every single day; no priest
would think against her, and her goodness was well known.
If she went to secret doings back there in the bush where the
full-bloods were, nobody said a word. Her fingers were always
busy with farm work or else the needle, thread, and Rosary.
People would recall her team and buggy and alongside her the
boy they called "Bay-riss." They went to pick seneca root and
peeled cranberry bark and sold berries to the farm wives down
on the prairie, he would jump down from the buggy calling in
his sweet voice, "O lay-*dees,* would you like to buy the bay-riss?"
He was the seventh son.

In those days and for years and years she would go down
to all the little towns and farms, all the way down to the train
station three days' journey from La Mountain. There she brought
her wares, selling baskets of berries and later many beadwork
things when she got too old and tired to forage in the woods.
After her horse and buggy days were over, around the time of
the Space Race, she caught a ride with the Interagency Motor
Pool on "official business" since a great-nephew was the driver.
When she was a girl the Sioux called her people the "flower
beadwork people" and she knew the Ojibway word for this art
implied the spirit in which such things were made.

Finally one day Angeline had sold all and there was still
not enough money for a winter cache of groceries from the
store, so when the lady on the eastbound train said *How bout
that? I fancy that clever little purse,* she thought, "I have outlived
everybody and the one I would give it to as a gift is not here
and never will be." Now here is the pale blonde daughter of

Le Septième, studying this odd museum artifact, reading its
description card and wondering, Why would an Indian make
such a thing as this instead of something more Indian? And
then *flashclick* she has a picture for her friend in the anthropology department back at college to try and figure out.

WOMAN'S PURSE
Tanned deer hide with flap and thong closure,
Lined with Bull Durham tobacco pouch.
Outer seams finished with white bead edging.
Green shamrock pattern on back,
Yellow heraldic device bordered in black,
random pattern of seven white beads on black velvet.
Beadwork.
H. 10.5 cm, W. 10.5 cm.
Collected in North Dakota, 1959.
Tribe unknown.

Lorena Fuerta ¤ Mescalero Apache/Yaqui

Untitled

Patriarchal

arrows

sharply chiseled

fashionmagazinedisplaymodels

aimed

closely fitted

tightshirtshortskirts

angledhipsandjaggedlips

enticing who?

My own daughter falters,

wounded by precision advertisement,

not understanding

the true purpose of the pictures,

weakened and attacked

yet still hoping to be chosen

in adoration

of

the

Hunt

Miracle

August 20, 1994. The white calf was born a week ago to a
rancher in Janesville, Wisconsin. It is said by many Plains tribes
to be apocalyptic. Right up there with all the natural disasters
going on around the world, starvation in third world countries
and the peace between nations that had warred for decades.
Native people were coming from all over to pay homage. The
white buffalo calf's eyes peered out from the rumpled newsprint.
Grace tore out the picture and pinned it up by the mirror. "Are
you the second coming?" she asked.

Grace threw down the paper after reading it. "I'm ready for
the end of the world," she sighed to her cat, Fishbone. She had
just been fired from her waitress job at the Big Top Deli. The
owner had waited to fire her until after she scrubbed the last of
the burnt nacho cheese from the pot. She had searched the
want ads but came up with nothing she was qualified for. She
threw her faded Pendleton blanket over her bed and fixed the
pillow over the worn spot.

Out on the street it was easily 102 degrees. Grace took her
old backpack and started off down the sidewalk. Melted, sticky
gum held to her sandals and pulled her back down to earth.
She felt sweat running down her breasts and legs. A hippie
man dressed only in tiny shorts and a headband passed her.
The smell of sweat and excrement trailed behind him. She
wanted to tell him how badly he stunk but changed her mind.
There was no way for anyone not to be sweaty on the humid
boulevard. The heat waves were coming up from the sidewalk
and even they had a stale odor. Her crucifix swung against her
chest and caused her to think again of the buffalo. She stepped
off into the street without looking and a loud car horn startled
her awake.

"I ought to get out and beat the crap out of your Indian ass!"
an old white man yelled at her.

"Get over it, you old fart!" she called back.

There were signs at the Urban Indian Center that proclaimed the building condemned for the past six months. The people working there had not located a new building that they could afford so they hadn't moved yet. The city had seemed to forget the signs anyway. On the creaky old second floor the job announcements were posted. Someone had written "Free Leonard Peltier" in a dozen different colors on the bulletin board. No job announcement suited her. There were twenty listings but each one called for bachelor's degrees in varying fields. There were listings for construction jobs. Grace didn't know anything about construction. She had holed away enough money for two more weeks. Maybe she would be able to collect unemployment.

On her way home she bought a bottle of red wine and some frozen fish. In the meat market, she thought she saw a white buffalo on an advertisement for fresh beef. She did a double take and took a closer look at the poster. Surely the store wouldn't use a picture of a white buffalo to sell meat. It turned out to be an ordinary cow with faded paint. This was becoming her obsession. She thought again of the white buffalo as she made her way down the street. There were some Indian guys lying on the ground outside of the Seven Sisters Bar. "Get up, you guys," she whispered across the street to them. "Wake up! The buffalo calf is here. It has come to save the people!" She moved on as the nearest one stumbled to his feet to cry out for her help. She wanted to pick them all up and take them home and bathe them and cook for them. She would show them the picture of the albino calf and tell them to have faith. Instead she was frightened of what might happen instead. "Hey, sister, gimme a quarter or thirty-seven cents," the staggering man shouted at her.

Roman was coming out of the building when she got back to her apartment. "Amazing Grace," he greeted her, smiling. "When you gonna let me take you to Mexico?"

"Hey Roman." She smiled back. Roman was always saying things like this to her. Grace had known him for a while and thought about asking him out. This was before he had shown up with Robin. Grace was disappointed when Robin moved in with him. Grace tried to be friendly but Robin didn't speak to her very often. Robin was very white with big hazel eyes. Roman and Grace were both dark with long, black hair. When they were hanging out together some people would look at them from behind and think they were both women. They would call Roman "Miss" and he would say dirty words in Kiowa to them. He would tell Grace what the words meant and she learned to say them. Once when they went for coffee, the waiters confused their orders. Roman told the waiter, "That's okay. All Indians look alike, enit?"

Grace admired his attitude. He often told her not to let other people's ignorance get to her. "Listen, one of the worst things anyone ever called me was 'white bread.' This was done by some Indian dude on the street. I'm not going to perpetuate ignorance by reacting to it. I got better things to do with my time."

He was packing up his van with boxes, sweat dripping into his eyes. He looked at Grace with one eye closed. "Robin's moving out for awhile." He turned and looked at the boxes. "I'm too tired to argue about it." Robin came down and gave Grace an irritated look. She threw a leopard-print bag into the back and said "That's it. Let's go."

Grace said goodbye to them as they got into the van. Neither one replied. She could see their angry mouths moving as they drove off. Grace went in and had her meal of wine and fish. She lay down on her bed to study the want ads. She fell asleep immediately.

In her dream her grandmother was coming toward her. She appeared to be on horseback. As she got closer, she actually became the horse. Grace called out, "Kah-koo!" The horse had feathers tied to its mane. It stepped up close to her. She felt the heat of its breath on her face. Then it turned and ran out of sight. Grace turned to go and found a small feather on the ground.

There was the sound of a yelping dog outside. Fishbone was startled out of his sleep and jumped to the window. Grace opened it and pushed him out. It was eight A.M. and overcast. She was surprised that she had lain all night on the newspapers without waking. There was a knock on the door. She ran her hands over her hair as she opened the door. It was Roman. "Hey Grace, I've got some coffee." She took the chain off the door and let him in. Roman eyed her disheveled clothing. "Aren't you going to work this morning? Or you got the afternoon? You should wash your face, you look a little crusty around your eyes."

He looked around the cupboards as she went to wash up. He found coffee filters and made them a pot of strong black coffee. He looked in the refrigerator and found an egg, some moldy bread and a beer. Grace came back in fresh clothes, combing her hair. "Man, you don't have any food. All I could find was a beer." He held it up and opened it.

"Well, help yourself, Roman," she said sarcastically. She opened a box that held two cans of commodity peanut butter and some boneless chicken. "I've got food."

Roman laughed. "Never mind about that. Hell, I'll take you out for breakfast. You're not taking very good care of yourself." She got up, got out two big mugs and poured the steaming coffee. She glanced at him sideways, wishing she had known he was coming over this morning. "Roman, you must be mighty bored without Robin around."

"No, actually what I wanted to tell you was that I'm going out of town and I needed a little help. I need someone to look after the place." Roman looked in the cabinet and found some sugar packets. He tossed some on the table and poured one into his cup.

"I'm going up to Wisconsin for a couple of weeks. They need some extra help workin' on a bridge. Think you could help me? Just take care of the plants, get the mail. You can have whatever food we have upstairs."

Grace had not heard the entire request. "You've got to be kidding! I can't believe my luck!" She took a big gulp of her coffee.

Roman smiled sheepishly. "Well, hell. Okay. You don't have to be so . . . Maybe I asked more than I should. I thought you might water the plants. There are only two of them. The cops confiscated the rest. Ha ha."

Grace wasn't listening. She bit her lip and thought. "You're going to Wisconsin. Don't you know anything? The white buffalo calf was born up there! I want to go with you. I won't get in the way, I swear. I need to go up there and see it for myself. I would help drive and whatever else. I have a little money. How about it?" Her eyes grew large with excitement as she thought. "Wait, what did you say about cops?"

"I said if you don't behave I'm gonna call the cops!" Roman smiled and shook his head. "I don't know. I might not even be going anywhere near . . . I don't know if you'd have a place to stay."

They pulled into Amarillo amid the stench of cattle. They bought gas, newspapers and drinks. It was already hot and humid. Their windows were down and flies were buzzing all over the van. Grace tried to force them out of the open windows. The back of the van was filled with tools and a makeshift bed. Roman played tapes of old pow-wow recordings. The music was a strange soundtrack for the scenery of old dilapidated buildings in the Texas ghost towns. The hue of the earth changed as they slipped from Texas into Oklahoma from a yellow green to deep rust red.

"Roman, I've got some good friends in Anadarko. How long do you think we got to spare?" They veered off into southwest Oklahoma and went through Anadarko. Roman bought some deer horn buttons for his jacket at McKee's Indian store while Grace made phone calls from outside. She couldn't get hold of any friends. "She was at Riverside with me. An old roommate."

They pulled into a campground at Tulsa around midnight. They ate crackers and cheese and drank pop. Roman slept in the front seat and Grace lay on the mattress and dreamed about something lost.

In her dream she felt that she lost an animal. If she didn't find it, it would be injured. It wasn't Fishbone; she was carrying him with her. She panicked and began running. What sounded like a bear crashed behind her. She suddenly couldn't move and the sound filled all her senses.

When she woke up the sun was beating down on her sweat-covered face. "Where are we? Are we in Kansas, Toto?" She climbed to the front passenger seat. "Roman, you haven't said yet. What do you think of the buffalo calf? Is it a returning spirit, like the Sioux people believe? Like a savior?"

Roman wiped his nose with his handkerchief and adjusted his sunglasses. " I wasn't brought up believing in a mystical buffalo or anything. You know, that's not my people, the Sioux. My ol' granddad used to talk about all buffalo being sacred animals but that's about as far as it went."

Grace stretched out her legs and rolled up her jean legs. "Do you ever wonder about the end of the world? I dream about it all the time. One time, I dreamed that I saw God, or what I think God would look like. It was so real, so vivid. There was all this tremendous amount of destruction going on in the background. Like mudslides and tidal waves. But I just kept looking up at the sky. Another time, I dreamed the same thing. Then all these angels came out of the sky in little spacecrafts, like warriors, golden warriors. I reached out to touch one, I was hiding under a stairwell or something, and the little angel cut my hand. It pierced it and it burned like crazy. Even when I woke up my hand still burned. What do you think of that? Do you think it means anything?"

Roman shrugged. He glanced at her legs. "I don't really believe in Christianity or anything. I believe in Indian ways. The wind, the stars, the four directions, and the Creator. Not angels and Jesus and all that. Now, if I only knew the whole story about this buffalo calf maybe I could understand why you're traveling all this way. I figure I'm old-fashioned. I like the old ways. I could have really gotten into that warrior stuff, you know?"

Grace looked out of the window and rolled her eyes. "Yeah, you could kidnap all the white women you wanted."

Roman laughed. "Same old Grace." His smile faded.

Grace narrowed her eyes and watched the farmland roll by. The colors of auburn, gold and pale green stretched on for miles, dotted with lush, full trees. She rested her head against the window.

They stopped to clean up and stretch. Despite her will, Grace dozed on and off. She was sorry the way her attempts at conversation with Roman didn't pan out like she planned. At least he was on the level, though. She liked that. She wondered if he thought she was dim-witted.

"You want to drive for awhile? Stop giving me the silent treatment." Roman reached over and tried to push her hair out of her eyes. They pulled into a convenience store and changed sides. He stretched and yawned. "Look, there's a storm coming. When you were asleep there were all kinds of warnings. Tornado. Smell that rain? It's coming."

She got out and they watched the clouds rolling in. She didn't like the low, wispy clouds above them. It was eerie, the feeling of total quiet, of absolute stillness. Suddenly, the wind whipped up and a piece of trash flew by, hitting Roman in the head. Grace laughed and broke the silence.

They decided not to drive anymore that day. There was a motel up the road, the store clerk said. They made up their minds to wait out the storm for the night. They pooled their money and got a room with two beds. It was beginning to hail when Roman went back to the store to get some cigarettes, fried chicken, and beer. He brought the food in along with a flashlight and a portable radio. Grace opened her backpack and started beading on a piece of buckskin. Roman fiddled with the television and settled on a movie. He came and sat beside her on her bed.

"What's that for, a key chain?" he asked.

"No, I'm making an offering." She pulled the string with her teeth.

"Here." Roman took out a pocketknife and cut the string. He lit a cigarette and changed the channels on the radio. Three funnel clouds had been sighted. The storm was surrounding them. It shook the small windows of the room and pelted rocks and debris at the door. The rain smell filled the tiny room along with the smoke and chicken.

Grace was watching the movie, saying a prayer and beading. The prayer was a blessing and a plea at the same time. Thunder shook the motel. The sky was a nasty yellow green. She hated tornadoes. Roman watched her. "I guess we could get under the beds anytime." He looked under the bed. "Along with the roaches and silverfish." He glanced at her. Grace was beading furiously, with deep furrows on her brow.

"Don't worry. The storm will pass." Roman walked to the window and looked out.

The power had begun to go on and off. Roman couldn't get a clear channel on the radio. He changed the television chan-nel and another movie flickered on. There were two women in an embrace. One began to slowly undress the other. Grace looked at Roman. He was totally engrossed. She looked back at the television.

She felt the hot, red flush of confused embarrassment creep up her neck. "For God's sake, please turn that off." She looked back at her beading.

"What? It's okay. It's pretty good. Plus, we're getting it for free!" He backed his way to the bed and sat on the edge. "Let me help you." He smiled and took her beadwork out of her hands and placed it on the bedside table. He moved toward her and smiled.

"Roman, we're friends. Just friends. We're in a motel room, and I . . ." He pushed her back on the plaid bedspread. She was startled. The needle she was still holding pricked her skin. She struggled to sit up. "Roman." She pushed at him. "Wait. Let me up!" Instead he held her even more tightly and kissed her. For a moment his warm mouth over whelmed any other thought in her mind.

Outside lightning struck the ground with a sharp, metallic crack and the power totally went out. There was some yelling outside the window. A small brush fire had started and two scraggly men were beating it out with burlap bags. Grace and Roman ran out and watched. One of the men eyed them. "Some storm, huh? You did a rain-dance, huh, chief? Looks like the storm is heading north."

Roman turned and went back into the room. The fire had gone out. Grace went up and asked the man how far it was to Janesville, Wisconsin. The man snorted.

"You Indians headed up to see the buffalo calf, huh? The miracle. Yeah, we went up and seen it. Nothin' special. You seen one, you seen 'em all. The farm is a good day and a half's drive away from here. Seen a lot of Indians goin' through." He made a motion to Grace's motel room with his chin. "The chief, where's he? He doin' a ceremony or what?"

Grace studied him for a moment. "He's not a chief," she replied. She walked back to the room and stood in the open doorway.

"Listen, Roman. This can't happen. You're still involved with . . . ?," she glanced at him and sat on the opposite bed.

Roman was sprawled out on the bed. He turned and buried his face in the pillow. "It's no big thing. " He turned over and kicked off his boots. "Hell, just forget about it. It's in the past already."

"Look, don't get mad. I'm just on this trip trying to make some sense out of life. I see the destruction of ourselves, the planet, children. Sometimes there seems to be no hope." She tugged at her t-shirt. She looked and him and smiled sadly. "My brain just won't leave me alone, you know. I don't even go to church but I worry about Catholic priests molesting people. I worry about women using abortion as birth control, those alcoholics passed out on the ground outside the bars. Hell, AIDS killed that man in the apartment next door." She wiped tears out of her eyes. "It just never ends and there's not a damn thing I can do about any of it. It just goes on and on."

Roman sat up. "Hold on now. Why do you think this is your entire problem? You think too much. Come here, please." He held out his hand.

Grace went over and sat beside him. "It's not thinking too much. It's not thinking enough, or not doing enough. Think about it. There's still starvation in the world. There's still slavery. How in the hell can you not think about all this? All the time, every day. Come on. Open your eyes!"

Roman started playing with her hair. He stroked her neck. "They are open. I don't need a sermon."

Grace got up. "I can't sleep with you. You still have a girl-friend. If you can't deal with that, well, I'll just get me a bus ticket back home."

Roman laughed. "What? Now just a damn minute. Go ahead and catch the bus if you want to. I just kissed you. I didn't say I wanted to go to bed with you." He laid on the bed and rolled up in the faded bedspread and faced the wall. "Go to sleep, Grace. We still have a long way to go."

The rain started again. Roman lay motionless. The power came on. The television blasted on and the same two women were now in a hot tub with a hairy man. Grace stood up and changed the channel to the news. Rain was expected all night. Roman sat back up.

"Wow, the power came back. Look, Grace. I'm sorry. I really thought that you wanted to fool around. I should know that a woman on a quest for the Holy Grail wouldn't be like that. I'll take you on up to your buffalo. We'll go first thing in the morning. Come on, Grace. I think about the end of the world and the whole mess. How could I not? But all we can do is do our best. You know what they say: God is Red. If that's so, then your buffalo should be pretty damn . . . should be pretty holy."

In her dream it was the end of the world. She was safe, just standing watching. The mudslides were throwing cars and trucks off the roads. The colors were bleeding into each other. The fire in the sky and the fire in the sea blended. Far across the river Grace could see her grandmother waving. She was holding a sacred ceremonial pipe. At her side was a young woman in white buckskin, a transformation of the calf. Grace looked back at the destruction of the earth. In the dream, it was Roman she was with. She threw the buckskin that she was holding, and the beads turned into a rainbow path. Dozens of others, people of every color, stepped onto the path and started across.

Linda LeGarde Grover ⋈ Ojibwe

Ikwe Ishpiming

From black of light years, asi anang

writhed and spiraled into his path,

shedding sparks that dazzled his eyes.

He raised his arm to shade his face

and began his dance, unaware that he danced

while above I flew, gold in the sky.

With my hair the wind I tethered his wrists

to a shining cloud, as I silently swayed

and breathed in the breeze, ambe, ambe.

My hands the earth that gave him life

bathed his feet in shredding silk

that tore in my touch as I whispered,

ambe omaa, bimosen, bimosen.

Then my lips rained silver sand that poured

into the river, that rolled from its sleep,

and I spoke through the water, wewib wewib,

til he followed, filling my tracks with his own.

⋈ ⋈ ⋈

To the Woman Who Just Bought a Set of Native American Spirituality Dream Interpretation Cards

Sister, listen carefully to this.

You'll probably go right past me
when you're looking
for a real gen-yew-whine
Indian princess
to flagellate you a little
and feed your self-indulgent
un-guilt
about what other people
not as fine-tuned and sensitive as you
did to women
by the way, women like me
who you probably go right past
when you're looking.

I know what you're looking for
and I know I'm not it.
You're looking for that other
Indian woman, you want
a for real gen-yew-whine
oshki-traditional princess
and you'll know her when you see her
glibly glinting silver and turquoise
carrying around her own little
magic shop of real gen-yew-whine
rattling beads and jangling charms
beaming about her moon
as she sells you a ticket to her sweat lodge.
She's a spiritual concession stand
and it's your own business go ahead and buy

or rent it if you want go ahead
what do I care
acquire what you will,
you've done it before.

I know what you're looking for
and I know I'm not it. Hell, no
I won't be dressing up or dancing for you
or selling you a ceremony
that women around here never heard of
I won't tell your fortune
or interpret your dreams
so put away your money. Hell,
what you really want to buy
you'll never see, and anyway
it's not for sale.

Sister, you weren't listening to this
I know, and I know too that
that authentic, guaranteed
satisfaction or your money back
gen-yew-whine for real
oshki-traditional Indian princess
is easy to find. Bring your checkbook.
Or a major credit card.
I'll be watching you both.

Teresa Iyall-Santos ¤ Coeur d'Alene/Yakama

Grandmother, Salish Mathematician

Grandmother, my *Yay-Yay*
made this dress with purpose:
for protection, for legacies,
for balance in our worlds.
Patterns evoked from song—
buckskin called to be her mode.

Ooo-Neh! Mathematics here is immense.
Measured dimensions hanging abstract,
cut-glass beads strung through thread
creating a matrix of geometry
symmetrical beyond belief,
its value absolute.

Yay-Yay knew these concepts,
constructed with brilliant hands.
Tonight dress lives through dance
moving through spaces magnetic.

Equations of perfect balance,
repetitions of patterns complex.
Yay-Yay + Spirit = Balance
balance infinite
in cyclical time.

Sara Littlecrow-Russell ¤ Anishinaabe/Han

Escape from the Rez on a Saturday Night

You sit across from me
in your Tommy Hilfiger half shirt
and your great-grandma's beaded barrette.

"This sucks, there's nothing to do."

Your lipstick sticky mouth
takes a last drag off your stolen cigarette,
as you get up to dance.

Skin-tight bellbottoms
strain against the muscles of your
Iroquois Smoke Dancer's legs—
10,000-year-old rhythm collides
with hardcore hip-hop thunder
as you dance hard
to make your place in a world
that does not welcome
you as an Indian,
but as a delectable
twelve-year-old girl.

All night I've been
watching the dopeman
as he watches you, waiting
for you to realize
the Rez is too boring
and you just want
something happenin' around here.

Marcie Rendon ¤ White Earth Anishinaabe

what's an indian woman to do?

what's an indian woman to do
when the white girls act more indian
than the indian women do?

my tongue trips over takonsala
mumbles around the word mitakuye oyasin
my ojibwe's been corrected
by a blond U of M undergraduate

what's an indian woman to do?

much to my ex-husband's dismay
i never learned the humble,
spiritual,
Native woman stance
legs tight, arms close, head bowed
three paces behind

my mother worked and fought with men
strode across fields
100-pound potato sacks on shoulders broad as any man
the most traditional thing
my grandfather taught me
was to put jeebik on the cue stick
to win a game of pool
so i never learned the finer
indian arts
so many white women have become adept at
sometimes i go to pow-wows
see them selling wares

somehow the little crystals
tied on leather pouches
never pull my indian heart

huh, what's an indian woman to do?

i remember Kathy She Who Sees the Spirit Lights
when she was still
Katrina Olson from Mankato, Minnesota
and Raven Woman?
damn, i swear i knew her
when she was a jewish girl
over in st. paul

as my hair grays
theirs gets darker
month by month
their reservation accents
thicker
year by year

used to be
reincarnation happened
only to the dead

hmmm?!?!?

what's an indian woman to do
when the white girls act more indian
than the indians do???

Annie Cecilia Smith ¤ Yakama

The Frybread Queen

Imagine you are at a powwow and you are looking around at
the Native American arts and crafts. While walking around
you smell heated vegetable oil. You see a lady yelling "Frybread!
Frybread!" You see her with floury, doughy hands making what
seem to be doughnuts. Well, you walk around some more and
see that there are several stands selling this frybread stuff and
decide to try one. After your first bite you're thinking in your
mind "Hey, this stuff tastes pretty good" and decide to try
another one. And yet another one!

What exactly is frybread? Frybread is practically a food
group for us Indians. Frybread isn't something you see in the
bread section of Albertson's or Safeway, rather you would see
frybread anywhere there is a big gathering of Indians like at
powwows and dinners. You see, us Indians have our own food
groups, divided up into four parts. The first section is our traditional foods (like salmon, elk, deer, roots, and berries). The
second section is frybread. The third section is commodities
(like cheese, flour, dried milk, canned vegetables, and all that
other good stuff). The final section is the "everything else"
group (like Pepsi, McDonald's, and whatever else can be found
at Safeway or Albertson's). This group speaks for itself.

So what's the big deal with frybread? Let's go back to that
frybread stand at that powwow. I am standing in line after you,
with your greasy hands and lips. After getting your third piece
of frybread, you say that it tastes really good and that it was
your first time you had it. Well, I take a bite and think that frybread is too thick, or too doughy, or too hard, or too burnt and
throw it on the ground and walk to the next frybread stand.
You see, frybread has to be perfect in every way. It can't be too
thick. It can't be too burnt. It can't be too doughy. It can't be too
hard. It has to be just right. If it's not, then it tastes "all right,"
and just "all right." This perfection of frybread making comes

not from the one who makes it but the ones who eat it. They tell the frybread maker what the flaws of the frybread are. That frybread will be one step closer to being the "best frybread."

That's what every one of us frybread makers want. We want it to be so good that it will be used at every bake sale, car wash, and bingo night. Instead of seeing little girls on the rez going door to door with Girl Scout cookies, they will be selling your frybread, because it is the best frybread.

Because your frybread is the best frybread you will soon be known as the "frybread queen."

Who cares if you're the frybread queen? Being a frybread queen is similar to being the president of the United States. Once a frybread queen, always a frybread queen. That name will stay with you for the rest of your life. Another example would be like getting a Ph.D. in frybread making from Frybread University. Now, I can't go right out and say why being the frybread queen is such a big deal. In a way, it's a joke between us Indians. It's not like you can go out to the rez and say "Hey, who's the frybread queen around here?" All of the women would probably laugh at you if you did ask for the "queen," but seriously, all of them would want to tell you that you're looking at her. It's the recognition that all Indian women want. (And even men, perhaps? That's a whole different story! Let's not even go there!) By being frybread queen, whenever you make your frybread, your frybread becomes "magic." Indians become happy when their bellies are full of some of your good frybread. Just like your families when you make your "specialty," they too become happy with your "magic."

I am still working hard for a degree in frybread making. Right now I'm probably a sophomore or junior or something, but I'm getting up there! Wish me luck! Some day I may put a frybread stand up at some little powwow on the rez or even during the Gathering of Nations powwow. After I've graduated from Frybread University, of course.

Love is Blind

One missing tooth

When he smiles

And I smile

His glasses

Held together

With duct tape

And I laugh

His two braids

Across his chest

Are so bushy

And I am cracking up

Tears run down my cheek

My stomach hurts

He made me frybread

And I fell in love

¤ ¤ ¤

Not Indian Enough

"My great-grandmother was a Cherokee princess. I'm one-sixteenth Cherokee," is what a proud, light-skinned, blond-haired person states to me. I want to laugh because it's not the first time I've heard such a claim. It seems that there's always this issue of "Who's Indian?" And if you are Indian are you Indian enough? It's a pressure all right, this business of being Indian.

Why do people tell me that their great-grandmother was a Cherokee princess? Or how much Indian blood they have? First of all there is no such thing as a Cherokee princess. Never was. Never has been. All of a sudden ZAP! And everyone's great-grandmother was a Cherokee princess. Is this magic or what! Might as well just tell me that their great-grandmother was Pocahontas or Sacajewea.

My guess is "they" say the Cherokee princess thing to prove that they are Indian. But it's obvious who the "real" Indian is, me. I am a Native American. And damn proud! I do the usual Indian stuff, you know, like the tomahawk chop. I wonder if the great-grandchild of a Cherokee princess would proudly say the tomahawk chop was a real Indian thing.

I own a rez car. My rez car is a 1985 Pontiac 6000. Left door is dented, so you can get in only on the right side of the car. The place where the back window used to be is covered with duct tape and plastic. The radio works, when it wants to. I open the trunk with an Indian key, a screwdriver. I have a tribal ID. This is similar to a license to drive. Only very useless. This is a license to be Indian. I know the songs of my religion. I eat fry-bread. Drink Pepsi. I say enit. I eat commodities. I just love that government cheese! What "real" Indian doesn't? I play basketball. I dance. I bead. I have long brown hair and brown eyes. How much Indian does that make me? If you don't know what any of this Indian stuff is, I already know your great-grandmother was NOT a Cherokee princess!

Still, there's a deeper issue of Indianness. Of course, there is no such thing as being too much of an Indian. I do worry about being not Indian enough. I don't know how to speak my language. Does speaking only English make me less of an Indian? I don't know many of the stories. Stories. Stories that tell my history. My past. If I don't know where I came from, how will I go forward and live life as a "real" Indian? Many, if not all, young people will say they are proud to be a Native American. Yet, they don't do much, if any, of the usual Indian stuff. How can someone be proud of something they don't know much about? Like many other youth, I am lost. I am a needle in a haystack.

Here's the "real" answer. It is not the White people nor the Indian people who measure how much an Indian really is— only you can measure how much Indian you really are. It's too bad that the only way that a person accepts being Indian is by saying that their great-grandmother was a Cherokee princess. Instead of telling everyone else that your great-grandmother was a Cherokee princess, or that you are one-sixteenth Cherokee, try this: tell yourself. The pressure of being Indian is worth it. I know. *I have been dancing ever since I've started to walk. Whenever I can, I travel to powwows near and far. I see many old friends and meet many new ones. We eat frybread and drink Pepsi. Hearing the singing and seeing the dancing awakens my soul.*

Kimberly Wensaut ¤ Potawatomi

Alina in Kansas

Alina Alina, lovely Lina
you are tucked away on the high Midwestern plains

between the Mission of mercy—
whose black robes wrote our ancestors' names in their
    baptismal books
quill strokes reshaping the Yellow Thunders into Johnsons
the Red Clouds into Jacksons

—and the wooden dance hall
whose singers' voices rise up the walls like prayerful smoke
remembering the people's names
drawing them close to the circle

Lina Lina, lilting Lina
you dreamed that rust weary car
would carry you across the country
like carriage under moonlight
like wagon under hot sun
tired horses anxious to please your small courage
which became immense
and filled the sky

Lina you found a home on the prairie
and there you sit
mending the holes in our memory moccasins
worn thin by the long march
from the shores of our Lake Michigan
and weaving the dusty threads
into colorful patterns
that will surely last another century

Lina Lina, little sister
I believe you have never told a lie
for it is you who appears singing
in the midst of my nightmares
your purity blanketing my dream horizon
like clouds fresh with rain
bringing showers to the thirsty
and trickles of laughter to forgotten spring holes

Venaya Yazzie ☐ Navajo

after powwow

one o'clock A.M.
and we stood in endless
flat
blackness
with the stars singing
in our presence.
with the stars shining
in our presence.

1:02 A.M.
and we talked
about that light-skinned northern girl
the one
with the blue and silver jingle dress
She looked like a movie star.
She looked like black and white photographs.

1:04 A.M.
a falling star.
It entered—
falling from the sacred direction
of Cassiopeia
and
we rolled a smoke it was the tobacco
offered at the
Smith family giveaway,
after grand entry
by that traditional dancer from pyramid lake.
the one

we both wanted to
owl dance with.

1:06 A.M.
with the missed forty-nine
on our
minds we sat in hypnotic silence
driving
on the blue highway.

1:30 A.M.
in town
our stomachs growl
with the loud city lights
and
we decided on the 24-hour
village inn restaurant
for cheeseburgers and pancakes
and talked with our shiny worded
friend with the beautiful Cree
smile.

two A.M.
and
we hugged
and we knew
we'd all meet again
next weekend at
some community center gym.

2:01 A.M.
the drive
back home
and
the new moon
reflected
the asphalt
on the blue highway
west; our bellies content and our
minds fed.

4 In the Arms of the Skies

As we read through the submissions for this book, Heid mentioned that in an Ojibwe story a woman leaves with her Star Husband to live in the sky. I told of Changing Woman who meets a handsome young man by the river; he turns out to be the Sun. She "marries" him and gives birth to the Twin Heroes. In the Navajo stories, when sky and earth meet, rain results to nourish the earth. You can appreciate the understated sexual imagery. A similar motif appears in the Yellow Woman stories of the Laguna Pueblo people, in which Yellow Woman meets a katsina by the river who kidnaps her. In other stories Sky Woman falls from the sky and creates a nation. Alongside these stories are those inclusive of romance and love in its varied forms. We decided to name this section "In the Arms of the Sky."

I don't know about other tribal languages, but in the Navajo language there are no terms of endearment for loved ones other than family and children. Terms of endearment might be taken from English and given with love, or with tongue-in-cheek expression, to a spouse or lover. Much of the work written about romantic love and sensuality is expressed within the context of landscape and animal imagery as they are in the works of kateri akiwenzie-damm, Vee F. Browne, and myself. Joy Harjo's "How to Get to the Planet Venus" brings a fresh interpretation of Sky Woman, with betrayal redeemed by the saving grace of love.

Then there are the stories that we Indian women know all too well, about relationships that are fickle, undependable, abusive, and unhealthy. Mothers advise against putting a man on a pedestal lest he betray the woman. Indian women talk of finding a "good Indian man" who isn't damaged from year's of walking on the edge of life's razor. Sara Littlecrow-Russell asks the proverbial question in "Is It Too Much to Ask?" I've heard cynical jokes that a good Indian man is one who hasn't lost all his teeth. Indian women know too well how addictions and the loss of traditions in the backlash of colonial imperialism have often wrought domestic violence, broken family relationships, and betrayal, sadly weakening Indian communities and nations.

Still, we find representations of sensual and erotic love in the body of work written by Native women, though they are few and far between, at least in the work that we received. Perhaps that is what prompted Sherman Alexie to ask, in *The Toughest Indian in the World*, "what Navajos looked like when they were naked and in love." Here are poems and stories of sensual love and relationships with mysterious and lovely beings, and sometimes with not-so-mysterious or lovely beings. Here are some stories that further express the dynamic dimensions of Native women.

Laura Tohe

kateri akiwenzie-damm ✳ Anishinaabe

the one who got away

babe
what words will lead you
to the inlet of my mouth

where your silence is becoming
trout
flopping on the sunbaked stone
of my tongue

zebra mussels take hold
spreading and clinging like sharp edged doubts
slicing the tender words
you sent
last month
last week

i pull away bleeding

last time
my hand reached out to touch you
hesitated in midair
like salmon jumping
in a photo
caught in a moment of light and darkness

before falling
battered against rocks

i hide in the shallows

grow thin

watch the seasons change

Esther Belin * Navajo

Emergence

I.
She was born out of his cuss words
and spittle
probably urine-matted floors gave essence
to his character
and now to hers
pumped through umbilical blood
her teeth grinding down his bad habits
his laugh
with deceiving smile
a possible caress
right before he guts
Ruby's mother with words
emerging from the bottom of his heel.

When Ruby met her mother
the only roots she could plant
were bitter and twisted and contagious.

From Ruby she wails.

II.
I often wonder
which Easy Street
he emerged
mother only calls him Fast Car
"That's all I remember,"
mother says passively
"It was that kind of love
you know
that some way
kind of connection. That

is how you were created."
My bet is a Capri
a Chevrolet Capri
deep, strong blue
not too green
solid blue with maybe some glitter
there was sparkle
from what info I can squeeze out of mother
there was sparkle
perhaps it was his eyes
that mixed-blood blue
sparkling through his eyes
or just maybe
it was his blue jeans
with that just-right fit
sparkling from his highly polished
Pro-Rodeo silver buckle
with real gold trim
I have seen that kind before
with pretty smile to boot
maybe it was the smile
How about a gold-rimmed smile
a front tooth laced with gold trim
sparkling from across
the pow wow arena
I hope he was at least
a lead singer
I hope from up north
I always wanted to go to Canada
perhaps there
I will find him
that Fast Car
that got away

or
ran away
whatever the case
I learned my lesson from that sparkle
that sparkle
so potent and tight
bound into a confined space of beauty
caustic with the least amount of heat
my body still glows from the explosion
Mother and Fast Car
What a sight!

III.
My birth began at thirty-two
from water to water
when mother was ready to birth
a consuming heat rushed her body
being the middle of winter
folks thought she was crazed
bobbing in and out of the waves on the beach
naked and alive with motion
people snapped photos
"An Indigenous Woman Returns to Ocean Homeland"
one headline read
"Indian Woman Commits Suicide on Beach"
was a popular thought
the salt water
the muse from the waves
were her doulas
all she says is
"Easy Street"
It's as if I just swam out of her womb
into the arms of another
sweet caress

One photo immediately after my birth
mother is just laughing
in bliss
watching me swim
still connected

IV.
I am still haunted
by the voice
or the hand
the one that slams
heads into dresser drawers
shoulders into doorways
hearts into heavy balls of clay
and the pounding would get stung
from the solid mass it created
defending with only the emptiness
not a sparkle of life
in sight
just a story
that shivers me
in my boots.

Old Man Jones said
he knew the man
mother called Fast Car
He'd begin
"From up north, I believe . . ."
The year he told me that story
I started to learn "O Canada"
the Canadian national anthem
I sang in the shower
on the school bus
when I was alone

Mother looked at me a bit strange
and I always thought
I pulled one over on her
and she'd just smile
thinking I was working on a school project
I even bought one of those Canadian flags
the kind with the Indian man
covering part of the maple leaf
AIM was big then
so on Independence Day
I sure raised that flag from our front porch
Mother never did budge
on offering any
Fast Car info
so I quit singing
and packed away that flag
by then it occurred to me
mother probably never
understood geography
and my need to locate
myself on someone's map.

Vee F. Browne　*　Navajo

Smile

Your smile is like a pale pink waterfall
around my lonely earth.

Your smile rules the "break of day,"
which draws the curtain of dawn
and lets in your sun rays.

An intriguing
smile sends a plateful of butterflies
piercing my "restless heart."

That sultry smile, that one
is like a Neapolitan rainbow
after a summer rain shower.

I sit against a fountain of happiness
after the mauve sunset pulls down
the black sky.

I think of your smile
night after day.

I
break the crystal silence
when I grin along with the falling stars.

Yidlohgo t'óó shił nizhóní yee'.

You've got to know that,
you release butterflies
sailing through my lonesome world.

Diane Glancy * Cherokee

The Great Spirit's Wife

He led the way up a great ladder of small clouds, and we followed him up
through an opening in the sky. He took us to the Great Spirit and his wife, and . . .
I saw they were dressed like Indians. Then he showed us his hands and feet, and
there were wounds in them . . .
> Kicking Bear in a speech
> to a council of Sioux, 1890

She must be small
her ears made of spools
unwound from the thread
you know over the sundance ground
you saw white threads heading west
the hot afternoon you lay on the ground
in the shadow of the tent
looking skyward for the Great Spirit's wife
maybe she'd stop peeling potatoes long enough
to look down and spit on you
her mouth so pure and cool it would be like rain.

*   *   *

The Abandoned Wife Gives Herself to the Lord

My heart is warm like fire, but there are cold spots in it. I don't know how to talk. I want to be a white man. My Father did not tell me it was wrong to have so many wives. I love all my women. My old wife is a mother to the others; I can't do without her, but she is old and cannot work very much; I can't send her away to die. This woman cost me ten horses; she is young; she will take care of me when I am old. I want to do right. I'm not a bad man. I know your new law is good.

Chief Mark considers monogamy
at the Warm Springs Agency, 1871

She felt dizzy with hunger. The spirits began to speak. She saw the Holy One on his cloud spearing something. He fished as if he had a claw and the salmon jumped to him. She sat on the rock waiting for him to see her. She'd heard his believers called the Bride of Christ. She knew he was a man who took more than one wife.

Joy Harjo * Muscogee Creek

How to Get to the Planet Venus

I used to fly to the moon. I never had to think about it; it just
happened. This was before I went to school and learned that
I needed a degree in aerodynamics to understand how to get
from here to there.

One night the moon was full, bright with an aura of ice
as earth headed toward winter. My father hadn't come home
again and my mother waited in front of the television, the
blue flickering glow turning her back and forth between light
and dark. It had become more difficult to leave for the moon
because I never knew what would happen, what he would do
to her.

The luminescent road to the moon was strong and familiar
as I made my way to the old man who was my guardian there.
We did not need words to talk. That night he took me to a
quarry of stones and we walked down to the edge where the
scrap pieces were piled together. Below it we could see the
world I had come from. Across town my father was coming out
of Cain's Ballroom with a blonde woman on his arm. They were
kissing and laughing. We could see my mother doze as the television screen blurred, and then the baby awakened and she
went to him, changed his diaper and held him close to her neck
as she turned the light on in the kitchen to make his bottle.

This was the first time we had come here to this place
together. I knew then that this would be the last time for a very
long time I would see the old man and I felt sad. We watched
the story as it unwound through time and space, unraveling
like my mother's spools of threads when I accidentally dropped
them. But I would not recall any of it for a long time.

I returned at dawn and my father showed up with smeared
lipstick on his white shirt and the terrible anger of a trapped
cat. Not too long after, my father left us for a dancer and my

mother immediately married a white man who didn't want children. I was sent away to Indian school.

The moon was a slender knife in the dark winter sky. We huddled in the ditch behind the boys' dorm, passing around a bottle of sticky sweet cherry vodka. It kept away the cold and the ghosts of sadness and after a few sips I was free. Next to me was the new student Lupita Bear. I had to keep from staring at her. She was beautiful. Her perfect skin was café au lait and her black eyes elegant like a sacred cat. She announced she had checked out the male population of the school since she arrived earlier in the week and was giving a report.

"... And what's the name of that Sioux guy with the geometric painting designs? With the nice smile and perfect back, always running touchdowns between classes?"

"John Her Many Horses," we chimed. We'd all noticed him.

"That one over there." (She motioned to Herbie Nez. He was Navajo and slim as a girl.) "He's much too pretty. I could eat him up in one bite!"

Herbie's hearing was like radar and tuned in to everything, even the songs and cries of spirits who hung around the school. In the past children had been dragged there against their will. He looked over at us and batted his eyelashes. We all laughed as we downed the next round. Then suddenly our party was over. The dorm patrol surprised us in the nearly moonless night and we scattered into the dark to save ourselves from detention, restriction, and being sent away.

I ran until I couldn't run anymore. By the time I made it back my roommate had already been caught and had been judged and tried and was packing her bags for home. She was the first that semester to be kicked out of the dorm for drinking. She was to be the object lesson for all of us.

Her family came after breakfast the next morning just as a light rain blew in over the mountains. We all watched appre-

hensively from the dorm living room as her father stiffly lifted
her suitcases into their truck to take her back to Dulce. When
she climbed in next to her mother and brothers and sisters,
she turned and waved a heavy goodbye.

That night Georgette Romero woke up the whole dorm.
First I heard her screams and then her running as she fled down
the hall towards my room, which was in the farthest wing.
Lupita saw everything, she told me later, because she was up
at four A.M. writing a letter to her mother. When Georgette
ran by she was being chased by a ghost the color of sick green.
Her roommates refused to let her back to their room and
burned cedar to dispel the evil. No one wanted the girl with
the ghost but since I had the only extra bed it was decided
she move to my room. That night and for many nights after
I stayed alert in the dark and didn't sleep, anticipating the
return of the ghost. Georgette managed to sleep soundly; she
knew I was keeping watch.

Now Georgette's books were all over the floor and her
plastic beauty case spilled over with make-up and polishes,
flooding the counter we were supposed to share. For hours she
scraped and rubbed off chipped polish on her nails then reap-
plied numerous thick coats, smelling up the room with polish
and acetone. She left used dabs of cotton and underwear scattered on the floor. At first I was amused at this alien creature,
told myself that she had made herself her own canvas, but she
was getting on my nerves. I spent more and more time in the
painting studio or sat on the fire escape listening to music.

One afternoon when I came in from school I couldn't hear
anything for the whine blasting from Georgette's favorite country station. I had just been summoned to meet in half an hour
with the head dorm matron, Mrs.Wilhelm, and after the weekend I had every reason to be afraid. I needed to think quick.
If I was kicked out I could not go home. I had to make a plan
about what I would do, where I would run.

"Hey, I need that!" Georgette gestured to me with her nail polish applicator as I turned down the volume, almost muting it. "I had a rough day."

"Peace," I said, turning up the music a notch, then opened the windows to let in some air and to relieve the panic. I wouldn't go back. I would kill myself first.

Across the way from the boys' dorm I could hear Herbie Nez practicing his guitar. He was my other eyes, my other ears and we shared a love for jazz, Jimi Hendrix, and esoteric philosophies.

"Our dark sides are compatible," I told him one night as we flew to Jimi's guitar, far from the dancers in the center of the gym, far from the school, from pain.

"Hmmmmm . . ." he answered. "True, as true as horses breathing clouds in winter."

"Perfect," I answered.

And then he laughed and I laughed. We fit, though he was born in a hogan and didn't speak English until he was sent to a Catholic boarding school, and I was born in a city, speaking English. My father's language was a secret he used to speak with his relatives, the ones who hated my mother. She looked white and her relatives had signed the treaty for our tribe's removal from our homelands. That treaty was still fresh though the signing was almost two hundred years ago. Herbie's spirit gleamed and spun and called to me to climb higher and higher. And with him I always could, fearlessly.

Georgette was in love with Clarence, Herbie's cousin from the other side of the reservation. Clarence was one of those shy-eyed Navajo men with big eyelashes and a tight, tapered back. He lived for rodeo, for the ride, be it with horses, bulls or girls. Georgette's mood fluctuated according to her sightings of Clarence. She had been trying to lure him all semester and he was the focus of all her beauty tricks.

"So Clarence didn't bite today?" I asked.

Georgette glared at me. "That Mexican girl better go back where she came from is all I can say," she snapped.

"You mean the opera singer." I answered. Lupita Bear wanted to be an opera singer, went the rumor, but the idea of any of us becoming an opera singer seemed so preposterous. It was wildly possible, just not likely. It was probable that most of us would become cosmetologists or car mechanics, move back home and have babies.

Sitting in the ditch last weekend she didn't look like an opera singer; she was one of us. She had laughed as we ran through the dark from the dorm police. I could still hear it, a trained laugh, and for a moment I could imagine her as an opera singer, far away from here on a stage where her looks and shine could amount to something. She was gorgeous and she didn't have to try. She was half-Mexican, her father from a tribe in Oregon I had never heard of until I came here. The word was this school was her last chance.

Last night Herbie told me that Clarence had made a bet he could have her within a week, that she would be easy. All the boys were watching to see what would happen, and were placing bets. "Did you place a bet?" I questioned Herbie.

"Of course not," he had answered. "However, I'm placing a bet that I'll have that Lewis Jim wrapped around my fingers by Saturday night."

"Yes, the most improbable candidate for your love in the whole school."

"I like a challenge," he quipped.

We laughed at the incongruity. Lewis was Clarence's best friend. He rode bulls and even looked like a bull. He was square to the earth and prided himself as a stud and would probably beat Herbie up if he caught Herbie staring at him in public.

Georgette didn't know about the betting and I was tempted to tell her, but as much as I was growing to dislike her I didn't hate her.

Lupita's singing pulled me up the hallway as I prepared to meet my doom in Mrs. Wilhelm's office. She was singing along with KOMA radio, on a signal that flew straight across the plains all the way from Oklahoma City.

I stopped to listen, with everyone else who was within hearing distance. Her voice was a living, breathing thing, like Jimi Hendrix's guitar, like Jackson Pollack's paintings. My father told me that some voices are so true they can be used as weapons, can maneuver the weather, change time. He said that a voice that powerful can walk away from the singer if it is shamed. After my father left us I learned that some voices can deceive you. There is a top layer and there is a bottom and they don't match. Like my stepfather's voice. The top layer was jovial and witty and knew how to appeal to those in power. The bottom layer was a belt laced with anger and terrible desire for the teenage daughter of his wife, my mother.

Everyone clapped when the song was over.

"Forget opera," I blurted out, "you can sing anything you want." Everyone turned to look at me, including Clarence who was leaning against the wall, pretending he was an innocent audience member.

"Hey thanks," she said warmly. "Do I know you?"

We had met at the ditch. Maybe she had forgotten, then I saw her eyes move sideways toward the dorm assistants who were listening to everything. We couldn't be too careful. Maybe she too was waiting for Mrs. Wilhelm.

"I'm Lupita, from the planet Venus," she told me, smiling, aware of her rapt audience of high school boys who all snickered when she made reference to the planet Venus.

"I'm Bonita, Creek from Oklahoma. Oklahoma is a long way from Venus."

Though she was my age she seemed suddenly older as she slid her hands self-consciously along her tight sheath skirt. Her nails were long and painted, the look Georgette strived for but would never get. In that small moment I felt sorry for Georgette. She didn't have a chance. And just as suddenly Lupita was sixteen again, a girl in need of approval and attention.

"Do you really like my singing?"

She glanced over at Clarence who gave her a shy dance of his eyes. It was obvious that Lupita had a thing for Clarence. There was a light that jumped between them, an electrical force so strong that it sparkled in the late afternoon sun. Who was after whom? I wondered.

"Lupita, can you move your admiration society outside?"

It was Mrs. Wilhelm. I had briefly forgotten about her. She motioned me into her office with her determined chin and sharp gray eyes. Suddenly I was afraid again. The door shut with a precise click. I sat at the table I had shined with lemon wax just that morning. My detail was to clean her office after breakfast before going to school. I did so diligently, with respect and fear.

"I have something I want to show you," she said. Here it is, I thought. I expected her to pull out last weekend's report detailing the ditch episode, or at least point out an uneven wax job; instead, she put a letter in front of me.

It was addressed to Mrs. Wilhelm and it was from my stepfather. I had no idea why my stepfather would write Mrs. Wilhelm or the school. I had never seen him write a letter to anyone. His routine was to come in from work at four, find a reason to hit me, then read the evening paper. My mother would hide in the kitchen cooking dinner, though she was tired after waitressing all day at the diner for the old lady from back East who ran the place.

Once I lost it. My mother was exhausted from working a double shift. My stepfather sat in his huge chair in the middle of the room, barking out orders. He yelled at my mother to cut his meat, to bring him another glass of iced tea. Then he snapped at her because she wasn't moving fast enough.

"Hurry up, bring me some more ice! What's taking you so long?" He had just asked her for something at the other end of the house just a few minutes before.

Before I could put the brakes on I said, "Why don't you buy her a pair of roller skates so she can get around faster?" I was belted, then grounded forever. But it was worth it, like a thunderstorm cleaning evil and leaving a satisfied land.

I took out the letter. The envelope had been opened neatly already by Mrs. Wilhelm with the electric letter opener I dusted every morning. He had used my mother's drugstore stationery and had written neatly, sanely, with blue ink in a voice of careful authority:

Dear Mrs. Wilhelm,

I am writing to you because I think there are some things you need to know about our daughter who is now a student at your school. We had quite a problem with her when she was in our home and could not control her. Watch out for her. She will lie to you and she will steal. She is not to be trusted.

I was not his daughter, he had never called me daughter, nor had I lied to him or stolen anything. Tears threatened but I refused to give him that satisfaction, even six hundred miles away. My face blushed, stung by betrayal. He was the liar. He was the one who had stolen, he had stolen my mother's life and was attempting to steal my chance of making it out of his house, his domain. I stuttered but nothing came out.

Mrs. Wilhelm told me, "This is what I think about this letter," and she tore it up into pieces and threw it in the trash can. I was stunned. It had never occurred to me that it was possible to be trusted over the word of a white man who belonged to the Elks Club. As I left her office I promised myself that I would not drink again. She had believed in me, had given me another chance.

That was the first shock. The next shock was walking into my room to find Lupita sitting on my bed while Georgette struggled to pull on my prized fake suede hip-hugger bell-bottoms. They were stuck at her hips. Everyone on our floor shared clothes though they usually asked permission first. Georgette had not asked.

"Excuse me!" I shouted over the radio just as she triumphantly snapped the top button.

"They fit," said Georgette smugly as she pushed a chair up to the mirror over the drawers and climbed to admire herself front and back. "Do you mind if I borrow them?"

I stole a look at Lupita, who was absentmindedly sifting through Georgette's box of polishes. "Aren't they a little tight?" I asked.

"No, they fit perfectly," she said. So, in the name of making friends with Lupita I momentarily let it go, wincing as I watched Georgette make furtive swimming dance movements as she watched herself in the mirror.

"Be careful, and you'd better not dance in them," I reminded her as she hopped down.

I was still blown away by Lupita's voice. Her kind of talent was rare and burned bright. She had a chance. The school was paying for private music lessons, she told us as Georgette pulled out her nail polishes and picked out what I thought was a horrible color for Lupita. Lupita humored her, but she was no fool. The music teacher, however, wasn't just teaching her to sing. She laughed as she told us about his wandering hands as he put his arms around her to demonstrate abdominal breathing.

"So where is your mother from?" I figured I might as well find out the answer directly.

"Venus," she said. "She's from Venus, so I come from the planet Venus." She was serious.

It was then I remembered the old man, and how I used to fly to the moon. I remembered the quarry of stones and my mother holding the baby. I remembered my father. I felt lonesome, like my belly was being scraped by the edge of sorrow.

She and I talked about everything, about our fathers, about the ability to fly in dreams. Georgette listened quietly as she painted Lupita's nails. She volunteered nothing. I told Lupita I wanted to paint, to be an artist. She told me that what she really wanted was someone to love her, a house and babies. And then she said nonchalantly to me as she looked sideways at Georgette, "What do you know about that Navajo boy, the cowboy with the eyelashes, Clarence?" She had perfect timing, the mark of a good hunter or singer. She paused, then said, "He's a good kisser."

I hated confrontation and leapt back to get out of the way. "He's spoken for," choked Georgette, who stood up quickly to face her foe, spilling acetone all over Lupita and my favorite pants. The whole room stank of rotting apples.

Lupita knew exactly what Georgette had been up to all along when she'd invited her to our room. I wondered if she knew anything about Clarence's bet, and wondered if and when and how I should tell her. Lupita picked up Georgette's sharp nail file and pointed it at her before she began filing away.

Georgette wasn't through. "You Mexican bitch!" she snapped. "Get out of here."

"This is my room, too," I added. "And she can stay. And by the way, please take off my pants."

Georgette glared at me as she quickly replaced my pants with her skirt. She kicked the ruined pants aside. "You're both sick," she snapped. "Nobody can be from Venus or anyplace else but here." She marched out of the room carrying her case of nail polish.

Later, I made my way down the sidewalk to the painting studio to get myself back together. When I painted, everything else went away: the deals for seduction, the sad needs for attention, the missing fathers, fearful mothers, and evil stepfathers. I could fly to the moon, to Venus too if I wanted. I understood

Lupita when she said she was from Venus. I was from somewhere far away, the other side of the Milky Way and would return there someday. I knew it, just as I knew I could count on cerulean blue to be absolutely cerulean blue when I spread it on the canvas.

The freeze from the approaching cold front fixed the stars to the dark sky perfectly in place. The powwow club was practicing in the gym and a song flew out the tall narrow windows toward the white shell moon. The moon leaned delicately toward the bright planet of Venus, framed by the graceful cottonwoods lining the sidewalk. I felt flawed, imperfect, but what haunted me was not flamboyant like Georgette's ghost. It was a subtle thing, a graceful force even, like the field of stars my family saw in the night as we stompdanced every summer. It was born of a kink of reason, that is, if there is such beauty, then why are we suffering here?

As I opened the door to the studio Herbie jumped me. I screamed, then when I recognized him we laughed. I chased him, then held him down, made him promise never to frighten me again. Then I told him everything, about Lupita, about Georgette, about Mrs. Wilhelm and my stepfather, about the moon. He walked around me as I talked and got out my paints. He was high on possibilities, on hope and smoke.

"No!" I told him, "no, I can't" when he reminded me that he came over to take me to the dance at the canteen. "Today I made a promise and I can't risk getting sent home again. And I need to paint." The incantations of The Doors wound through the campus and through the door of the studio, tempting me.

"You're running from yourself. You're hiding from reality. Let's go, let's face everything together . . . Besides, I need you to check somebody out for me. Aieeeeeee."

It was Lewis Jim. And when I thought of Lewis Jim I remembered Lupita and the deal Clarence had going. Tonight was the deadline. I had to find Lupita and warn her before it was too late. I knew she had plans to go to the dance. That decided it.

The canteen was jammed. Herbie pulled me immediately out onto the dance floor. Dancing was like painting, like flying. Through rhythm I could travel toward the stars. Herbie and I could stay on the dance floor for hours and if we stayed in the canteen and danced I couldn't drink or get into any other kind of trouble. While we danced I kept my eyes on the door for Lupita. We danced every dance until a Mexican song interrupted and all the Apache girls flooded the dance floor.

While they weaved back and forth Herbie bought us Cokes and I looked around the room for Lupita. I didn't see her anywhere, or Clarence either. Georgette stood near the glass doors of the entrance. She looked small and alone as she borrowed a cigarette and lit it. I remembered the night she had upset the whole dorm with her panicked run from the ghost chasing her, and the big stink her roommates had caused when they demanded she move from their room. It wasn't just the ghost, they had charged, she was from an enemy tribe. No one had wanted a girl with a ghost in their rooms. I didn't want the ghost either but I felt sorry for the girl with the scratchy army blanket draped over her shoulders. The ghost had stayed away, but the fear kept following her.

I spotted Clarence coming up out of the dark, from the direction of the ditch. He was smiling and laughing a little too hard, walking with Lewis. Lupita wasn't with them. Clarence grabbed Georgette a little roughly. She smiled and melted into him and then they came into the door of the dance, Lewis following behind them. Georgette beamed with her prize and made sure I saw her.

"Where's Lupita?" I demanded. A knot crawled up my stomach. Georgette glared at me.

"She's on Venus," said Clarence and he and Lewis laughed. I didn't like the sound of their sly laughter.

I pulled a reluctant Herbie behind me. "We have to look for Lupita," I urged. He slid out the door of the packed canteen behind me.

"Wait, wait," he protested as he stared back at Lewis, who had no idea Herbie was interested in him. But Herbie was no fool. He knew better than to reveal his attraction as he pantomimed his broken heart behind Lewis's broad back.

We found Lupita almost immediately. "Over here," she called brightly. She waved us into the shadow between the painting and drawing studios. She was alone.

"Okay, Venus," joked Herbie. "This better be good. I just left the man of my dreams to come and look for you."

Her eyes shone as she pulled a pint of Everclear out from under her jacket.

"You guys go ahead," I said. "I'll sit this one out." I was trying to be good. It was then I saw the rough smudge of dirt on Lupita's jacket, the dainty lace of twigs on her thick black hair, and the bruise decorating her wrist. I thought of Clarence and Lewis walking smugly into the dance. It was more than I could bear. I took a drink and then another.

I lost track of time. One minute we were all back in the canteen dancing in a line to "Cotton-Eyed Joe" and then the next we were sitting under the moon out near the ditch with a stranger from town we'd hired to make a run for us. The earth was spinning and we were spinning with it. As we leaned into the burn, Lupita told us about her life, about how her mother had died when she was ten and left her with her father. She told how her father would tie her hair up every morning with her mother's ribbons before they left to work the fields together.

Herbie showed us the scar on his back made by a man who beat then raped him for his girlish ways. He made it sound funny but I didn't laugh. I didn't say anything; I was numb and flying far away, listening to the whir of the story as it unwound beneath the glowing moon.

Herbie disappeared somewhere in the dark and I could hear him throwing up. Someone was singing round dance songs. A dog barked from far, far away. Lupita had drifted into the bushes for what seemed years when the warning bell sounded from the girls' dorm. The sky was still spinning, but I willed myself to walk, step by step, to find Lupita, to make it back to the dorm in time. I looked for her through the blur of stars and sadness. I lost her. Without warning I remembered the stacked stones. I saw the unraveling story as it spun through time and space. And I saw what the old man had shown me that I hadn't been able to recall until now—how each thought and action fueled the momentum of the story—and how vulnerable we were to forgetting, all of us.

The final bell rang and I barely made it to my room, where I summoned a bit of soberness to save my life. I brushed my teeth so I would not smell like a drunk.

"Breathe," said the dorm assistant whose job it was on Friday and Saturday nights to go to each room and smell each girl's breath for alcohol. She stood poised with her pen, ready to make a mark against my name. I admired her clean life. Her parents showed up every weekend to bring her chili and fresh bread. She always stayed on the safe side of rules. I breathed. Then breathed again easily when she marked me present and sober.

No one had seen Lupita. Georgette floated into the room. "By the way," she said coolly, "Mrs. Wilhelm is looking for you. She wants you to come to her office."

I was still drunk when I entered Mrs. Wilhelm's office, though I had learned to hide it well. Lupita was sobbing and falling apart in front of a stern and disappointed Mrs. Wilhelm. "I want to go home. I want to go back to Venus," she cried as she buried her face in her arms.

I had failed not once, but twice. I had failed to warn Lupita in time and I had failed the trust of Mrs. Wilhelm who was the only person who had ever stood with me against the lies of my stepfather. Now Lupita would get sent home, not to Venus but to the father who had been sleeping with her since she was ten.

"Were you with Lupita tonight?" Mrs. Wilhelm sternly asked me.

What Mrs. Wilhelm was asking was whether or not I was drinking with Lupita. Immediately I thought of Georgette, the snitch. She had told. And maybe Mrs. Wilhelm didn't know, maybe she did. I couldn't tell for sure. But I knew that's not what really mattered. The truth became a path clearer than anything else, a shining luminescent bridge past all human failures. I could see the old man on the moon who always demanded nothing less than the truth. I had missed him but he had returned, as he had promised.

I confessed, "Yes, I was with Lupita," and I knew terribly that I was most likely dooming myself back to the house of my stepfather.

"Go take care of Lupita," Mrs. Wilhelm said. "I will talk with the two you tomorrow when you are sober." Then she slapped us each with a month of restriction. So she could keep a closer eye on us, she said.

I led the sodden Lupita back to her room. All night I held her while she cried for her mother, for home. All night, as we flew through the stars to the planet Venus.

Heather Harris * Cree-Métis

Coyote Meets His Match

Trickster, Transformer, Changing Person he's been called
Sometimes a person, sometimes a coyote
Sometimes neither, sometimes both
Hard to pin down, that Coyote

Coyote may not be wise
In a considered sort of way
But he's wily and resourceful
When he wants to get his way
And he has the power
To do most anything he sets his mind to

Coyote can fool most of us most of the time
But there's one he can't con
One he and all the other Coyotes can't deceive
One who understands him too well
One wise enough to be one step ahead of him at all times
That one
Is his mother

* * *

Husbands

Husbands
I had me a few
Easy to attract
Easy to keep
Hard to put up with

My mother
She had her a few
Tired of all of them

My grandmother
She had three
Dreamed one time
She stuffed them all in the furnace
Should have

Husbands come and go
Mothers, sisters and daughters last forever
A certain logic to matrilineality

Roberta Hill * Oneida

Elegy for Bobby

Listen. I'm carving a cleaner moon,
one without shadows, one that won't disappear
like you did on the other side of the sky,
one in whose full orange reflection
I'll see you walking down Seventh Avenue,
like you did those February days when grime
got the best of us. Your voice on the phone,
its breathy pauses like you just said something
that surprised you too, hung in the air
of my green house near the creek on Ray Road.
Back then, I drove through rain, leaving
my minuscule rez on a whim to wait
in some grim bar with wide brown siding
and yellow neon signs. Just when
I gave you up for good, you showed,
looking up as you came through the door,
taking a final drag from your cigarette,
your wary black eyes brightening my drink
like zesty shots of lemon. When you saw me,
the quizzical way your straight brows furrowed
moved me so much, I stayed every time.

Listen. You didn't have to go that way
into coma, letting paint make toxic
combinations of light and shallow breath.
Back then, I gathered your stalwart strength
in my arms. The way you stood made it seem
you would take life in your artist's hands forever.
You planned to paint each canvas blue, wanting
the color for rescue, like it did when you were five.
Remembering a precise moment on the porch
when cerulean breathed its truth,

you wanted to drink color, air and distance
like the true grace it is. Through you, Bobby,
that color found our world.
One moment in those fumbled meetings,
you sized me like a painting in progress. I touched
your rough face. Its fragile rhythms warmed
my hands with words. What plied
beneath our alcoholic haze was not love,
we laughed, because a bull and an octopus
could never fall in love. Ah, why did you have
to go that way?

Listen. I'm dreaming a deeper self,
one beyond stubbornness and judgment.
My impetuous inky energy disciplined
by strife, my awareness crisp as the snap
of a sheet, my heart raw and soft,
I remember how intense your life became,
how you painted the plains
as if cantilevered to the sky.
We've got the spaces you gave us,
delicate as puffs of breath in winter,
strong as the blue stars in Vela
smoky bright in a field glass.
The moon still rises. The creeks still flow.
Wet trunks darken with February rain.
I would have waited again to offer you
the hope that is also our heritage.
Now my unsettled hands simply miss
your beauty, whorled like a shell
beneath this mere current of words.

*   *   *

The Power of Crushed Leaves

Jack denied the ways he loved
before he came into her living room.
Marlene hid from him a hundred years,
because he made the hinges of her jaws ache
and her forehead shine with sweat.

Whether he drove gravel roads around the reservation
or pitched a tire iron into the glass
of an enemy's car, she was tuned into where
he might appear. Because he was forbidden,
she dreamed of him constantly.

Because he was forbidden, Marlene bore
longing like a moonflower, openly quaking
in predestined dark. Her stomach
thrilled with the thought of his arms
around her, his scent, the spice of sun on stone.

The path from ear to collarbone,
from collarbone to navel jangled her so intensely,
she dished all the fried potatoes to her brother,
had nothing left for Jack, her brother's oldest friend,
stopping by again like smoke in summer.

Night comforts both a babe and a stone
with indigo-stained hands. Night gave Jack a glance
that stopped birds in midair. For luck, he rubbed
his neck with the medicine of crushed leaves;
so old-fashioned, few talk about it now.

His scent charged the shadows in her soul
making her brave her father's sure displeasure.

Marlene took two years to find that field of sun,
where dittany, rattlesnake master, horse mint
and blue hyssop grew. Which one, which one?

By then his lovemaking kept her quaking
on cliffs of pleasure. She found
where the real din of him began, the man
who got her by the nose, she teased, snuggling
in the anise-scented breeze of his warm arms.

Sara Littlecrow-Russell * Anishinaabe/Han

My Books & Your White Women

When I am in pain
I want to run to you
like a wounded deer
that lies against the earth
driving the arrow deeper.

When I am in pain
I want to go home
to a place that smells
of sweetgrass and tobacco
the smell of you.

When we are together
all things are fine
Indian man, Indian woman
you bring me meat—I cook it
and when our bellies are full
we wrap ourselves
in your star blanket,
feed juniper roots to the fire,
and listen to the coy-dogs
chasing the evening train.

All things are good
until that other world intrudes
with burdens heavy
as shopping malls on burial mounds.

Each time we hug
my books and your white women
are between us.

Is It Too Much to Ask?

We're sitting at a powwow
washing down frybread with diet Pepsi
pretending that we're really
watching the dancing
but really we're just watching
the Indian men.

There are so many beautiful men in the arena
but in Ojibway there are many ways to say
something is nice to look at
and it's not always a compliment either.

A dancer with a bristling
bustle of eagle feathers
poses for the tourist cameras,
his hands subtly stroking a stranger woman's
sweaty, bare, white rolls of fat.
"He paid money for those eagle feathers,"
I say under my breath.
You laugh.
"Ego feathers."

An intertribal is called
and the arena fills with
flashes of brown skin and strong legs
through the somber trade cloth
of the Traditional Dancers
and the fluorescent whirl
of the Fancy and Grass Dancers.
I am in love and I am angry.
"Is it too much to ask?
An Indian man who's

not a drug addict
kind to living things
has half a brain or more
a reasonable amount of teeth
and is not young enough to
be my kid or old enough
to be my grandfather?"
You look at me like
I've just asked the
dumbest question in powwow history.
"Of course it is."

Laura Tohe * Navajo

The Big Rectangle

And what if
I were to accept your invitation
to slow dance up the stairs
 and find myself facing you in
   the big rec tangle

the slow descent
into desert mouths

legs
 curling,
  my vine growing next to yours

hands running smooth like deer leaping to their dreams

 I follow you into the summer evenings
 and wait for the world to open her arms
  to step inside
 we are eager for the breeze
 we are eager for the rain
 we are eager for the night

I'm happy you still wait for me by the river
 my water jar overturned

it doesn't mean I'll mend your sox
  iron your shirts
  birth your sons
     tell you to take the trash out

I want your touch,
    your damp palm of sand
        to swirl around me
     want you to light the sky
      with a candle
   lover, let me hear your wind voice moan
    blow sand into my doorway
     speak our language
   speak the possibility of traveling on rainbows

    I give you my warrior self
     you give me your warrior self
    it can't be any other way
    we move into the wet world
    thick and eager as salmon

*   *   *

Tsoodził, Mountain to the South

   You arrive in the bright of morning
   carrying music in your eyes
   and the breath of mountains in your hair

   We travel the path of thunder beings
   passing above stories where Twin Heroes slayed monsters
   proof lies in the dark mounds of lava trails
   streaming south from Tsoodził
   near the meadow where spring begins and calls forth
   yellow horses to graze among the cattails

I would tell you, beloved, these stories
on nights when the scent of orange blossoms lingers in the air
would tell you how brave locust smoothed the earth for humans
stories congealed into landscape
and how places mark existence

I want to travel all the colors of the worlds with you
to arrive in this Glittering World
held in your swollen male clouds
and your hand on my thigh
that causes the world to grow
again and again
without fine,
without end
your sweet music
pouring forth like
      rain
           rain
                rain
                    rain . . . .

Eulynda Toledo-Benalli * Navajo

Ashkii Nizhóní

"Always ask what someone's clan is," Grandma, Shimá sání,
said. My Bízhí, paternal aunt, would know who was my clan
and who wasn't, so she could tell me whom I could dance with.

Here I am, all dressed in good jeans and boots and a tight
top. My mom and dad wouldn't like my little top, but my excuse
is that it's too hot outside—Albuquerque is a hot city. The strong
air from the air conditioner feels good blowing my hair, keeping
my head cool. My hair, the best part of me, down to my butt—
feels good brushing my elbow when I move my hips. I wouldn't
want it any other way, like having to go to a beauty salon and
getting it all permed. Cowboy hats of all shapes, sizes, and colors
are going up and down and round and round on this dance floor.
Underneath the hats are almost stiff, moving bodies.

All the men notice this bleached blond, almost white-haired
woman with tight, tight Wranglers, flat, flat stomach, huge
buckle, and crotch noticeable from here. Some ladies like to
wear real wide, pleated skirts with their cowboy boots and like
to be swirled by their partners so their dresses fly up and you
could see their whole legs.

"Oh, no! Wasted!" my cousin Genevieve would say, if she
saw these women. Genevieve with her thick, short, permed
hair and rose-tinted glasses would be quite disturbed by these
women. Genevieve grew up about thirty miles away from me
and is quite a bit older. But she still liked going out to town
with me when I went dancing. Shizhé'é yázhí, my uncle,
Genevieve's father, would tell us all the medicine plants that
grew nearby our homes. It was he who brought herbs to my
mom every time we got sick. He instructed us on their use.

I could feel the music now in my boots, my pink ropers.
They go with the pink neon-shaped woman in a cowboy hat
with Dale Evans boots on the wall. At least it appears she has

clothes on, and at least the image is not that big. Underneath, that guy is looking at me a lot. He looks good in those tight Wranglers and that hair—a little long, a little curly, coarse, and black—hanging out of his Stetson. He might be Navajo—then I'd have to know his clan. He can be from any tribe, but please God, not Mexican or Chicano. My grandpa Shi Chee called them Nakaiłbáhí—Mexican gray. I don't know why he called them that but it just meant to me that they were not one of us.

The shot glass, cold and heavy, pours Jack Daniels down my throat, burning into my stomach. How can I sit in this dark bar and pretend I have no clan and dance like that and laugh so loud and forget my empty refrigerator back at my apartment? And that guy with tight Wranglers looks this way, too much.

Back on the rez, when I was younger, my Nálí, at my paternal grandma's Enemy Way ceremony, my Bízhí would point out to me who I could dance with. This was the only social part of the four-day ceremony. A dance that the whole community came to, with a huge fire crackling in the middle, which usually began after midnight. This is the Navajo "war dance." A time to confront the Enemy that is taking my grandma "out of balance"— that is why she is sick. By participating in my grandma's Enemy Way ceremony, all people would return to balance, even if it's just for that moment in song and dance.

I followed my Bízhí's instructions on who to dance with: someone who didn't share clan relations with me. It is the women who select their partners. You don't have to say, "May I have this dance?" You just go over to the guy and pull on his shirt. They say if he refuses, you can take his nice cowboy hat away from him. He also must pay you after he dances with you. That night I made a lot of money for my age. Something like twelve dollars and a few cents. My favorite partner was an old man with an old buckskin moneybag that had silver conchos which shone in the firelight. He gave me a dime and a penny from his bag.

But this guy, this Ashkii Nizhóní—Handsome Guy, doesn't have silver conchos. He has a shiny, well-made silver ranger buckle on his stamped leather belt. I could see it from here.

Soon I am dancing with Ashkii Nizhóní and the black walls swirl pink and silver and I am happy, I am embarrassed, I'm lucky. We dance and dance and laugh and laugh and he holds me by my waist.

Why should I tell him my name? I just laugh and say it's not important.

At the pink bar, he asks me where I'm from while my friend Bob is telling his story. I tune in a little harder to Bob's story. I laugh a little harder at Bob's joke about his "rez car"—only two doors, mustard yellow, parked outside with Arizona plates. We all laugh this time about his "war pony" that has no dashboard. Ashkii Nizhóní understands this "pan-Indin" humor. Maybe he's well traveled. A rodeo guy. I hope not. But then again, I could always brag about it.

That buckle of his looks like heavy silver with Navajo designs. Lots of people like Navajo designs. Wonder where he got it? A girlfriend, or his mother, or is this his own great taste?

I'm too silly for him. He's calm, he moves good, and he irons his western shirt. He drinks Cokes, that's all. What now? I see Steve in the corner laughing and grinning hard with his hand on this white woman's knee and she loves his bone and brass choker. How can he? How can she? "Gross!" I could hear my cousin Genevieve say. I want to choke Steve with his choker and tell the white woman to "get a grip." Looks too weird—Steve's long black braids and that red "layered-look" hair of hers. She looks like one of those that like to twirl. I know Steve would have too much to drink if he ever starts twirling her. Now I wish Genevieve was here so we could make up our stories and laugh.

I can smell Ashkii Nizhóní's expensive cologne now so I dance this time, more freely. I'm not gonna care. I'm not gonna ask.

The band takes a break. I haven't even noticed them. It's too quiet. Somebody, put something in the jukebox. I need pretzels. I could see my lonely bag of half-eaten pretzels in my empty cupboard. I eat a lot of those—crunchy, low fat, lot of salt and filling. I think I'll buy a bag. But they might get stuck in my teeth and ruin my smile.

He asks, "Where you from?" He attempts a Texas drawl, or is it Oklahoma? His voice as clear as the smell of burnt cedar. I am told the winds come in from the top of our heads and come out through our breath and words. We must be careful what we say. He is very careful. I don't get how he is able to blend his words like cold fresh spring water flowing over rocks.

"I'm from Crownpoint," I say. He must understand the high, lonely and alive desert I come from. Lots of sagebrush. That certain sagebrush that can't grow here in this hot, low city. The sagebrush that I miss especially when I walk by it and pinch a little with two fingers, like my mom does. Then I smell the most startling and safe wisp of earth's breath.

His eyes so dark brown, I don't want to know where he's from. He could be from Canada. Yeah, we're related to the Sarcee up there. He could be from Montana and a bull-dogger. No, I'd have to check his muscles first. He doesn't tell me.

"*Blame it on Texas! Don't blame it on me . . .*" the jukebox begins to blare. "*I am what I am and that's what I'm gonna be . . .*" That last line is the part I like.

I think I better get lost. I look for my girlfriend. There she is, dancing the Cotton-Eye-Joe with Benson from Oklahoma. Benson's a chef at the Holiday Inn. Boy, he dances good. Now they're yelling, "Bullshit!" I'm thinking sheep dip. Does this Ashkii Nizhóní know about sheep dip? If he saw me helping my father with the sheep dipping? I tried to look good in my best old clothes. The smell of our dipped sheep made me realize that was not my favorite job.

I go over to Benson and link arms, joining in. Too crowded

now, I kind of look for Ashkii Nizhóní. He's not sitting there
anymore. My feet begin to ache; it's time to go home. Maybe
it is best, the way it has happened.

*

Three weeks later I see him at the El Morro Restaurant. I want
a green chili burger real bad, and he, just a cup of coffee and a
cinnamon roll. I tell my girlfriend, "Remember him?" and she
pushes me to sit with him. We sit across from him at the red
vinyl booth.

I look outside on the street wondering what to talk about.
Nothing. A blind man and his dog walk by.

Ashkii Nizhóní tells me he's Navajo too. Man, I like the way
he talks. I look for the blind man and his dog. They are crossing
the street. He says, "What's your clan?" I tell him. He tells me
his—his Navajo so perfect. He doesn't know or show that our
clans are related. Real close. I know 'cuz my mom told me.

"Jus-sick!" I could hear my cousin Genevieve who already
has her cowboy.

I was dancing with my brother! My brother now holding a
coffee cup with rough, beautiful hands. My brother with a different Stetson and slight curls hanging out. I tell him, "You are
my brother," looking at my watch bracelet and sipping my Coke.

Shitsilí daats'í nílí, shinaí dats'í?—my older or my younger
brother? Our eyes lock for one second. We don't want to know.
He just smiles—barely, and I look away. I say, "No wonder you're
so good-looking. Everyone in our clan is always good-looking."
We laugh.

My girlfriend gets real interested. She doesn't have to worry.
She's from Laguna. The blind man and his dog walk by again.
Looks like one of our sheep dogs. We always had sheep dogs.
Shizhé'é, my father, always said they sense things we can't.

Then why couldn't Sam our sheep dog help me out with
this coyote? This coyote brother of mine. Crazy me. I could hear

them scolding now, my grandmas, my grandpas, my uncles, and my aunts. I guess I chose to be blind and refused to be led by a smart dog.

I need to get some gum, I say. I finally choose Juicy Fruit at the glass counter. I go to the postcard rack and look at each postcard, with each new picture on down the vertical holders on the rack. Pictures of Indins "war dancing." Kiowas probably. Pictures of Zuni ladies with pottery on their heads. "Olla maidens," somebody named them. And of course the usual postcards of "stuck-in-the-desert-with-rattlesnakes" pictures.

I look at my watch again. This time noticing the Navajo wedding basket background design. "Our universe is in this basket," my uncle says. "Everything that we are and where we come from is told through this basket."

The universe turns back into gold watch hands. It's time to get back to work. Gotta pay for my truck so I can go home on weekends and help haul wood and water for grandma.

I go back to Ashkii Nizhóní and stick my hand out to shake his hand, properly. "Hágoónee', ya." It's time to go. I turn to my girlfriend who looks all happy. "Let's go, girlfriend." We leave and I know I'll meet him again somewhere, and this time he will be my relative.

Kimberly Wensaut * Potawatomi

the way around losing you...

is a blond boy named joey with a white kawasaki
who I fall in love with
over hills through valleys
ocean wave sun and sky blue
and when do we get to go *really* fast i asked?
and i wanted to Give him my necklace, saw it
shining there on his tanned neck, shimmering
below his clear eyes and resting below
his perfect white teeth
blond boy could own my kickapoo necklace
sewn bead by bead by sarah in kansas, another world kansas
who is Married and is Small but hunts deer and skins them too
and i wonder, when did she cut off all her hair?
silken raven head and become tomboy? and how did she Find
a husband? in kansas? other world kansas?
when i have not and keep looking and meanwhile convince
     myself
i have fallen in love with another White Boy, White Boy
who is kind, kind, kind but has a woman already
so i keep my yellow red orange white and blue kickapoo
     necklace
knowing the way through twisted valleys dense and woody
     earthen smell:

my heart is only a metaphor for the way the earth holds
     her secrets
in the Sonoma valleys
my breath only imitation of her scent
in her ocean side hills

Contributors

kateri akiwenzie-damm, a Band member of the Chippewa of
Nawash born in Toronto in 1965, received an MA in English
literature from the University of Ottawa in 1996. She has lived
and worked in Neyaashiinigmiing (formerly the Cape Croker
Reserve) on the Saugeen Peninsula in southwestern Ontario
since 1994. Her writing has been published in various anthologies, journals, and magazines in Canada, the U.S., Aotearoa,
Australia, and Germany.

Of her home in Neyaashiinigmiing, she writes: I know I belong here
and regardless of where else I might live, this will always be my
home. This is where I live and write and remember who I am.

POETRY: *my heart is a stray bullet* (Kegedonce Press, 1993).

Esther Belin (Navajo) was raised in Lynwood, California. She is
among the myriad of indigenous peoples on this planet who
survive in urbanized areas. She graduated from the University
of California–Berkeley and Institute of American Indian Arts
in Santa Fe, New Mexico. Her work work has appeared in *Neon
Pow-Wow* (Northland, 1993); *Song of the Turtle* (Ballantine,
1994); and *Speaking for the Generations* (University of Arizona
Press, 1998).

POETRY: *From the Belly of My Beauty* (University of Arizona,
1999).

Kimberly Blaeser (Anishinaabe) is an enrolled member of the
Minnesota Chippewa Tribe and grew up on the White Earth
Reservation. An associate professor of English at the University
of Wisconsin–Milwaukee, she teaches courses in Native
American literature, creative writing, and American nature
writing. Her collection, *Trailing You,* won the 1993 First Book

Award from the Native Writers' Circle of the Americas. Her poetry, short fiction, personal essays, and scholarly articles have been anthologized in over sixty Canadian and American journals and collections.

Of "Shadow Sisters" she writes: This piece honors the many enduring relationships between woman on Indian reservations throughout this continent. It offers one chronology among the many sister stories—stories of our mothers and our aunties, our cousins and our own sisters. Native women still work at minimum-wage jobs to feed their families. They share work and child rearing, they support one another, and they carry the family and tribal stories. They live common, unselfconscious lives, with little time for the luxury of revolution. National news stories like the AIM (American Indian Movement) occupation at Wounded Knee or the Native Quincentenary observance of survival 500 years after Columbus are far removed from the day-to-day reality of these women. And yet, to the strength, humor, and anger they embody, we own our every survival.

POETRY: *Trailing You* (Greenfield Review Press, 1995); *Absentee Indians* (2002). CRITICAL STUDIES: *Gerald Vizenor: Writing in the Oral Tradition* (Oklahoma, 1996). ANTHOLOGY: *Stories Migrating Home* (Loonfeather Press, 1999).

Vee F. Browne is from Cottonwood/Tselani, Arizona, and is a member of the Navajo Nation. She belongs to the Bitter Water and Water Flows Together clans. She is a journalist, educator, volleyball and basketball referee, and fiction writer. An award-winning author, she has received much acclaim for her children's books. Browne's short stories have appeared in *Neon Pow-Wow* (Northland, 1993) and *Blue Dawn, Red Earth* (Anchor Books, 1996).

CHILDREN'S BOOKS: *Maria Tallchief* (Simon & Schuster, 1995); *Owl Book* (Scholastic, 1995); *Monster Bird* (Northland, 1993); *Monster Slayer* (Northland, 1991).

Elizabeth Cook-Lynn was born at Fort Thompson, South Dakota, and is a member of the Crow Creek Sioux Tribe. She is a recipient of an Oyate Igluwitaya award given by native university students in South Dakota, an award which refers to those who "aid in the ability of the people to see clearly in the company of each other." Since her retirement from Eastern Washington University, Cook-Lynn has been a visiting professor and consultant in Native American studies at the University of California–Davis and Arizona State University. Her many awards include the Myers Center Award for the Study of Human Rights in North America in 1997. She has been writer-in-residence at several universities and lives in the Black Hills of South Dakota.

FICTION: *Aurelia: A Crow Creek Trilogy* (Colorado, 1999). POETRY: *I Remember the Fallen Trees: New and Selected Poems* (Eastern Washington, 1998). NONFICTION: *Anti-Indianism in Modern America: A Voice from Tatekeya's Earth* (Illinois, 2001); *The Politics of Hallowed Ground: Wounded Knee and the Struggle for Indian Sovereignty* (Illinois, 1998; co-author with Mario Gonzalez); *Why I Can't Read Wallace Stegner: A Tribal Voice* (Wisconsin, 1996).

Pauline Danforth is from the White Earth Reservation, although she currently lives in the Twin Cities where she is writing her dissertation in American studies and working as an advisor to American Indian students at Metropolitan State University. Her prose has appeared in *Stories Migrating Home* and other anthologies.

Susan Deer Cloud is an award-winning writer of Mohawk, Blackfeet, and Seneca background who grew up in the Catskill Mountains. A recipient of a New York State Foundation for the Arts Poetry Fellowship, she has had poems and stories in numerous literary journals and anthologies. She teaches poetry writing at Binghamton University.

She writes of "Doe Season": In my tradition, women are the center of life and people give thanks to any animal they have to kill in order to feed themselves. Both animals and women are honored and admired—and considered "beautiful" in truest sense of word.

"Welcome to the Land of Ma'am": I always regarded the elders in my family as being beautiful in all ways. I didn't see them as "less" because they had lived here longer; I saw them as more. They were the ones with the stories in their shining faces and the stories on their glitter-tongues. They were the ones who gave me my life of stories and poetry. So I looked in my mirror of spirit one day and released a wolf howl and a war whoop— then transcribed my cries of defiance and affirmation in "Welcome to the Land of Ma'am."

"Her Pocahontas": This poem came out of a Christmas gift that my mother gave to me when I was a very little girl. This was the first doll I ever remember having and my mother told me that the doll's name was Pocahontas. She told me that the doll was Indian the way she was and I was.

POETRY: *In The Moon When The Deer Lose Their Horns* (Chantry, 1993); *The Broken Hoop* (Blue Cloud Quarterly Press, 1988).

Nicole Ducheneaux was born in Falls Church, Virginia, in 1978. She is an enrolled member of the Cheyenne River Sioux Tribe and has strong cultural and familial ties to her mother's tribe, the Confederated Salish and Kootenai. While pursuing a degree in history at the University of Maryland, she is working at a

Planned Parenthood clinic. What little free time she has is unwisely spent. This is her first publication.

Heid E. Erdrich was raised in North Dakota where her parents taught at the Wahpeton Indian School. She has degrees from Dartmouth College and the Johns Hopkins University. Her first collection of poetry, *Fishing for Myth,* won a Minnesota Voices Award in 1995 and was nominated for a Minnesota Book Award in 1998. A member of the Turtle Mountain Band of Ojibway, Erdrich teaches Native American literature and creative writing at the University of St. Thomas in St. Paul. Her current poetry manuscript is *The Honey Guide,* poems on childbirth. She is co-editor of *Sister Nations: Native Women Writers on Community.*

POETRY: *Fishing for Myth* (New Rivers Press, 1997).

Lise Erdrich is a Turtle Mountain Chippewa. Her fiction has been included in various journals and collections, including *The North Dakota Quarterly, Special Report: Fiction,* and *Tamaqua.* In 1989 she was the recipient of the John Hove Creative Writing Fellowship from the North Dakota Council of the Arts. Her short, "XXL," won the 1996 Tamarack Award from *Minnesota Monthly.*

Louise Erdrich is of German and Anishinaabe descent and is a member of the Turtle Mountain Band of Ojibway. Her many awards include the National Book Critics Circle Award for *Love Medicine* and three National Book Award nominations, most recently for *The Last Report on the Miracles at Little No Horse.* Her mother, Rita Gourneau, is a noted Ojibwe artist. Her sisters are the writers Heid Erdrich and Lise Erdrich, and her brothers Louis and Ralph work in the hospital system at Red Lake, Minnesota. Angela Erdrich, her youngest sister, is an Indian Health Service physician.

FICTION: *The Last Report on the Miracles at Little No Horse* (HarperCollins, 2001); *The Antelope Wife* (HarperFlamingo, 1998); *Tales of Burning Love* (HarperCollins, 1996); *The Bingo Palace* (HarperCollins, 1994); *Tracks* (Henry Holt, 1988); *The Beet Queen* (Henry Holt, 1986); *Love Medicine* (Holt, Rinehart and Winston, 1984; New and Expanded Version, HarperCollins, 1993). NONFICTION: *The Blue Jay's Dance: A Birth Year* (HarperCollins, 1996). POETRY: *Baptism of Desire* (Harper and Row, 1989); *Jacklight* (Holt, Rinehart and Winston, 1984). CHILDREN'S BOOKS: *The Birchbark House* (Hyperion, 1999); *Grandmother's Pigeon* (Hyperion, 1996).

Lorena Fuerta is of Mescalero Apache and Yaqui descent. Her home is in her writing, for it is in the stories of the people that she finds her existence. She was born in California and eventually joined the Air Force Reserves as an aircraft engine mechanic, later transferring to the Arizona Air National Guard to become an in-flight refueling specialist. She lives in Arizona with her husband, their cats, Sachi and Dinah, and their horse Shahla. Her poetry has been published in *Red Ink*.

Diane Glancy is of Cherokee and English/German heritage. She received her MFA from the University of Iowa. Her numerous awards include a National Endowment for the Arts grant, the Pablo Neruda Prize in Poetry, the North American Indian Prose Award, and the Wordcraft Circle of Native Writers Prose/ Playwriting Award. She teaches Native American literature and creative writing at Macalester College in St. Paul.

She writes: First of all, I'm interested in the voices of Native women, though they often seem to be historical voices. "The Great Spirit's Wife" was written on the Sun Dance grounds in South Dakota. "The Abandoned Wife Gives Herself to the Lord" was written in response to the difficulties of one belief system understanding another. I remain interested in the junction of

Christianity and tradition that somehow got put in the car trunk along the journey.

Several years ago, I saw an exhibit called, "Passionate Visions: Self-Taught Artists from 1940 to the Present," a collection of folk art using house paint, model airplane paint, tar and whatever could be found, on scrap metal, cardboard, tin and other materials. I wanted to go back and retrieve the primitiveness that was in my family. The texture of old voices. How do you relate the Native to America? Pick up what was left after the continental divide of language. I wanted to use the thought patterns and rhythms from the mix of two worlds I have experienced. Put them together in a new way. The walking in both worlds on one's own. The Cherokee and White. Old conjurers of tribal magic, the missionaries and circuit preachers.

Both poems are from a new collection of work called *Primer of the Obsolete.*

FICTION: *The Mask Maker* (University of Oklahoma Press, 2002); *The Man Who Heard the Land* (Minnesota Historical Society Press, 2001); *Fuller Man* (Moyer Bell, 1999); *The Voice that Was in Travel* (University of Oklahoma Press, 1999); *Flutie* (Moyer Bell, 1998); *Pushing the Bear* (Harcourt Brace, 1996); *The Only Piece of Furniture in the House* (Moyer Bell, 1996); *Monkey Secret* (Northwestern University Press/TriQuarterly Books, 1995); *Firesticks* (University of Oklahoma Press, 1993); *Trigger Dance* (Fiction Collective Two, 1990). NONFICTION: *The Cold-and-Hunger Dance* (University of Nebraska Press, 1998); *The West Pole* (University of Minnesota Press, 1997); *Claiming Breath* (University of Nebraska Press, 1996). POETRY: *Stones for a Pillow* (National Federation of State Poetry Societies, 2001); *The Relief of America* (Northwestern University Press/Tia Chucha Press, 2000); *(Ado)Ration* (Chax Press, 1999); *The Closets of Heaven* (Chax Press, 1999); *Boom Town* (Black Hat Press, 1997); *Lone Dog's Winter Count* (University of New Mexico Press, 1991); *Iron Woman* (New Rivers Press, 1991); *Offering* (Holy Cow! Press,

1988); *One Age in a Dream* (Milkweed Editions, 1986). DRAMA: *War Cries* (Holy Cow! Press, 1997). ANTHOLOGY: *Visit Teepee Town* (Coffee House Press, 1999; co-editor with Mark Nowak); *Two Worlds Walking: Short Stories, Essays, and Poetry by Writers with Mixed Heritages* (New Rivers Press, 1994; co-editor with C. W. Truesdale).

Terry Gomez is a Comanche from Oklahoma. She is a playwright, writer, artist, actor, director and producer. Her paintings and sculpture have been exhibited in several shows, and she has performed in several staged readings and plays. Her work has been published in the anthologies *Home Is in the Blood* (Institute of American Indian Arts, 1995); *Gathering Our Own* (Institute of American Indian Arts, 1996); *Contemporary Plays by Women of Color* (Routledge, 1996). Other work has been published in *Aboriginal Voices* magazine. Her play "Inter-Tribal" was presented as a staged reading at the Public Theater in New York City, as well as full production in Santa Fe, New Mexico. She lives in Santa Fe with her children.

Reva Mariah S. Gover, AKA Mariah Gover, is Skidi-Pawnee and Tohono O'odham. She is the writing instructor for the recently established Tohono O'odham Community College in Sells, Arizona. A single mom for a very smart little man-child, she tries diligently to balance work, family and some space to write a little poetry, sometimes a bit of fiction. She still enjoys pow-wows, 49s (when she can find one), good music, and laughter.

Linda LeGarde Grover is a member of the Bois Forte Band of the Minnesota Chippewa Tribe and an assistant professor in American Indian studies and education at the University of Minnesota Duluth. She believes that an Indian poet is a witness to and recorder of history who interprets experiences and writes so that our children and grandchildren will know and remember what is important to our survival as a people.

She writes of "Chi-Ko-Ko-koho": Memories of the Indian boarding school experience, though often repressed, surfaced at unexpected times long after students left school. Chi-Ko-Ko-koho encountered his boarding school prefect, tangibly or intangibly, years after the experience.

"Dream Interpretation Cards": New Age efforts to acquire Indian culture and spirituality by purchasing power is observed by an Indian woman in line at a bookstore. We have lost so much; can we risk losing more for money?

"Ikwe Ishpiming": The relationship between man and woman is as old as our memories and stories.

Debra Haaland is an enrolled member of Laguna Pueblo, New Mexico. Her family circle extends from Jemez Pueblo in northern New Mexico to Norway, where her great-grandparents lived before coming to the United States in 1880, the year the railroad went through Laguna. She received a BA from the University of New Mexico in 1994 and an MA in American Indian studies from the University of California–Los Angeles in 2001. She lives with her daughter Somah in Santa Monica, California.

Of "My Mother's Love," she writes: Part of my story resulted from stories of my mother growing up in the Indian Camp in Winslow, Arizona. Before my grandparents returned to Laguna Pueblo in the late 1960s, I had spent many summers with them in Winslow. Although they had bought a house and moved away from the Indian Camp by the time I was born, it remained ever-present both in conversation and proximity—my grandpa continued to work only a stone's throw away from the boxcars where he raised his family.

Another profound period of my life happened during the summer of 1998. I had stayed close to my great-aunt in and out of an Albuquerque hospital until her daughters took her home for the final time. It was there that I learned a great deal, from my cousins, about how to care for an elder person. I witnessed an unconditional love that I had never seen before or since. Spending hours in the hospital made me realize how little commitment or literally how few family members one has or can count on at the end of their lives. My aunt's case was far different from those other patients around her. Her room was always filled with family, laughter, love, and most importantly, familiarity.

Given these two circumstances, my story explores how a daughter reconciles a history of abuse by realizing that her mother did, indeed, love her. The overarching lesson through the pain and discipline was the mother's desire for her daughter to aspire to perfection, because she loved her. In finally realizing this at the end of her mother's life, the daughter has no moral, intellectual, or emotional choice but to never leave her mother's side.

Joy Harjo is a Muscogee Creek, born in Tulsa, Oklahoma, in 1951. Her many honors include an American Book Award, the Delmore Schwartz Memorial Award, the American Indian Distinguished Achievement in the Arts Award, the Josephine Miles Poetry Award, the Mountains and Plains Booksellers Award, the William Carlos Williams Award, and fellowships from the Arizona Commission on the Arts, the Witter Bynner Foundation, and the National Endowment for the Arts. She also performs her poetry and plays saxophone with her band, Poetic Justice. She lives in Albuquerque, New Mexico.

She writes of "How to Get to the Planet Venus": This story is one of a series of stories I am currently working on, of young Indian women coming of age in the late sixties and early seventies.

The first story of the series was completely autobiographical. I crafted it like a short story. The next was predominately fictional, the next more fictional. I am now at work on the fourth. I like the challenge of craft of narrative as well as the challenge of the craft of being human. These stories are also meant to be useful, to engender more stories from others, especially young Indian men and women.

POETRY: *A Map to the Next World* (Norton, 2001); *The Woman Who Fell From the Sky* (Norton, 1996); *In Mad Love and War* (Wesleyan University Press, 1990); *Secrets from the Center of the World* (University of Arizona Press, 1989); *She Had Some Horses* (Thunder's Mouth Press, 1983); *What Moon Drove Me to This?* (I Reed Books, 1979). CHILDREN'S BOOKS: *The Good Luck Cat* (Harcourt, 2000). ANTHOLOGY: *Reinventing the Enemy's Language* (Norton, 1997; co-editor with Gloria Bird).

Heather Harris is Cree-Metis born in British Columbia. For many years she lived among the Gitxsan from whom she has received considerable teaching and influence. She teaches First Nations studies at the University of Northern British Columbia, where she is completing her Ph.D. in anthropology. She is married, has three children, and is a visual artist and traditional dancer as well as a poet.

POETRY: *Rainbow Dancer* (Caitlin Press, 1999).

Allison Adelle Hedge Coke is Huron, Tsa la gi (Cherokee), French Canadian and Portuguese. She received an MFA from Vermont College and an AFA from the Institute for American Indian Arts. Her writing has been included in many journals and magazines, as well as the anthologies *Speaking for the Generations and the Lands* (University of Arizona Press, 1998); *Reinventing the Enemy's Language* (W. W. Norton, 1997). She received an American Book Award in 1998 for *Dog Road Woman* and was named the Mentor of the Year in 2001 by the Wordcraft Circle of Native Writers and Storytellers for her work with incarcerated Native youth.

She writes of "In the Fields": This is an excerpt from my survival narrative (memoir) *Rock, Ghost, Willow, Deer.* This excerpt is pulled from my coming of age as a Tsa la gi female in our homelands, North Carolina, where we sharecropped tobacco; planted corn, sweet potatoes, squash, and beans; fished, hunted, played music, and created whatever we needed to survive, to entertain ourselves, and to enjoy life. These years were some of the most engaging of my life.

POETRY: *Year of the Rat* (Grimes Press, 1999); *Dog Road Woman* (Coffee House Press, 1997). ANTHOLOGY: *Voices of Thunder* (Institute of American Indian Arts Press, 1992; co-editor with Heather Ahtone); *It's Not Quiet Anymore* (Institute of American Indian Arts Press, 1990; co-editor with Heather Ahtone).

Inés Hernández-Avila is Nimipu (Nez Perce) of Chief Joseph's band on her mother's side and Tejana on her father's side. She is enrolled on the Colville Confederated Tribal Reservation. She is an associate professor and former chair of the department of Native American studies at the University of California–Davis. Her poetry has appeared widely in such venues as *Americas Review, Poetry East, Flyway, Gatherings: The En'owkin Journal of North American First Peoples, Wicazo Sa Review, Callaloo,* and the anthology *Reinventing the Enemy's Language.*

Roberta J. Hill (Whiteman), an enrolled member of the Oneida Nation of Wisconsin, is a poet, fiction writer, and scholar. She earned a BA from the University of Wisconsin, an MFA from the University of Montana, and a PH.D. in American studies from the University of Minnesota. A professor of English and American Indian studies at the University of Wisconsin, she has received a Lila Wallace–Reader's Digest Award, among

others. Her poetry has been selected for inclusion in the
St. Paul Poetry Garden and the Midwest Express Convention
Center in Milwaukee. Her fiction, poetry, and essays have
appeared in a number of anthologies and magazines, most
recently in *The Beloit Poetry Journal,* and forthcoming in *Luna*
and *Prairie Schooner.* She is completing the biography of her
grandmother, Dr. Lillie Rosa Minoka-Hill, the second American
Indian woman physician, to be published by the University of
Nebraska Press.

POETRY: *Philadelphia Flowers* (Holy Cow! Press, 1996); *Star Quilt*
(Holy Cow! Press, 1984).

LeAnne Howe is an enrolled member of the Choctaw Nation of
Oklahoma, born in Edmond, Oklahoma. Raised and educated in
Oklahoma, she received her MFA from Vermont College and cur-
rently teaches Native Literature, the fiction workshop at Wake
Forest University, in Winston-Salem, North Carolina. Her fiction
appears in numerous anthologies, including: *Spider Woman's
Granddaughters, Earth Song, Sky Spirit: An Anthology of Native
American Writers, Global Cultures: A Transnational Short Fiction
Reader,* and *Reinventing the Enemy's Language.*

FICTION: *Shell Shaker* (Aunt Lute Books, 2001); *A Stand Up Reader*
(Into View Press, 1987); *Coyote Stories* (Wowapi Press, 1984).

Teresa Iyall-Santos is of Coeur d'Alene/Yakama ancestry. Born in
Spokane, Washington, she was raised with the cultural traditions of her mother's people, the Coeur d'Alene. She graduated
from Western Washington University, majoring in English literature and theater arts, and received her MA in education, specializing in creative arts and learning. She is an elementary
school teacher and lives with her husband and two daughters
in Silverdale, Washington. This is her first publication.

She writes of "Grandmother, Salish Mathematician": As a student in high school and in college I had always struggled with math. It wasn't until later in my own educational career that I began to learn about teaching to different learning styles and then began this practice with my fifth grade students. In doing this, the fundamentals of mathematics began to make sense, opening doors for me to learn even more difficult concepts. This also led me to look back to the traditions of my tribe, the Coeur d'Alene people. I thought of my grandmother and realized she was, indeed, a gifted mathematician. She was a terrific problem-solver, capable of the abstract thinking that was relative to her world.

I have seen Indian student test scores decline, often scoring the lowest of ethnic groups in the areas of math and science. We have got to teach in ways so our students are able to make these concepts relative to their world.

In writing "Grandmother, Salish Mathematician," I used sensory and linguistic modes. I held the buckskin dress sewn by Yay-Yay, my grandmother. It's heavily beaded, with shapes created into beautiful geometric patterns. In the other hand I held my daughter's algebra book opened to the glossary. The two connected.

Winona LaDuke grew up in Los Angeles and is Anishinaabe from the Makwa Dodaem (Bear Clan) of the Mississippi Band of the White Earth reservation in northern Minnesota. After graduating from Harvard, LaDuke moved to White Earth, where she became involved in a lawsuit to recover lands originally held by the Anishinaabe and taken illegally by the federal government. After exhausting options in the legal system, she founded the White Earth Land Recovery Project in order to raise funds to purchase original White Earth land holdings. She was the recipient of the 1989 International Reebok Human Rights Award and was named as one of "Fifty Leaders for the Future" by Time magazine in 1995. Among her many other activities, she was Ralph Nader's vice presidential running mate in the 1996 and 2000 presidential elections.

FICTION: *Last Standing Woman* (Voyageur Press, 1999). NONFIC-TION: *All Our Relations: Native Struggles for Land and Life* (South End Press, 1999).

Sara Littlecrow-Russell's poems have appeared in *American Indian Quarterly, Red Ink, The Massachusetts Review, Hip Mama, Race Traitor Journal, Femspec, Survivor,* and in Winona LaDuke's book, *All Our Relations: Native Struggles for Land and Life.* She is Metís and a single mother of two. Recently she received a degree from Hampshire College. Her work focuses on domestic violence prevention and community conflict resolution in Native America. She lives with her children in Boston, Massachusetts, where she attends Northeastern Law School.

Linda Noel is a native Californian of the Konkow Maidu tribe. She has been writing poetry for most of her adult life and has been published in anthologies and journals throughout the country. She is employed at Consolidated Tribal Health Project, Inc., as the community educator.

She says of her work: In many of my pieces I make reference to stitch or stitches and I don't mean suture. The term *stitch* refers to basket stitch and how we are woven into this life, pressed into this circle-shaped world through the stitching of our parents, grandparents and all ancestors, all relatives. Maybe this world is a big basket, ever evolving into its roundness and our individual lives are the designs and of course a circle. Every breath, every word, every day, every poem another stitch contributing to the roundness and the beauty and belief in tomorrow.

Suzanne Rancourt, born and raised in West Central Maine, is
Abenaki, Bear Clan, and served six years in the United States
Marine Corps and three in the United States Army. She is an
internationally published writer, a mentor for the Wordcraft
Writers' Circle, a singer-songwriter who has performed nation-
ally, and an independent education consultant. Suzanne holds
an MFA in poetry from Vermont College and an MS in educational psychology from State University of New York–Albany.
She is the parent education specialist for a Head Start Program
in northern New York. As diverse as the Natural World itself,
Suzanne is a personal fitness trainer, percussionist, herbal educator and not too shabby a dancer. She is a dance teacher and
member of the Yellah Shakina Shakti Middle Eastern Dance
Troupe specializing in Ethnic World Fusion.

She writes of "Sipping": Much of the living in the Northeast, even
now but especially for my mother's generation, focused on self-
sustenance and just plain survival. A common transition for
many Indian people. People did, and still do for the most part,
do what they gotta do to survive. Butchering your own animals,
hunting, and agricultural farming were a fact of life. I have
many memories of stories, realities, and a particular way of life
that was changing drastically as I was growing up. I remember
hearing cows being called: "Com' boss! Com' boss!" Switchel,
poor man's ginger ale, is a field drink made from vinegar, ginger, sugar, and water for long days of bringing in hay. I still mix
up a batch in the summer just because. I will always recall the
time I was sitting in the halls of academia and the professor
read a Greek pastoral poem where the heifers got milked. I
laughed so hard tears literally ran down my face and when I
realized that no one in the class knew what I was laughing
about I darn near wet myself. Although my generation was
moving into "modern" living, how we lived ethically main-
tained the old ways of country lifestyles including respect for

the natural world and the resources. Nothing was taken for granted. Survival meant living harmoniously within a community. When I wrote this poem for my mother it was to acknowledge and to honor the bittersweet victory of survival. The poem is about a way of life that was god-awful hard but honest. There simply wasn't time for anything else. And yet in all that hardness there was always a sense of family and a joy for being alive. I miss blunt honesty almost as much as I miss my mother.

Marcie R. Rendon, White Earth Anishinaabe, is a mother, grandmother, writer, and sometimes performance artist. A former recipient of the Loft's Inroads Writers of Color Award for Native Americans she is a 1998-99 recipient of the St. Paul Company's Leadership In Neighborhoods Grant to "create a viable Native presence in the Twin Cities theater community." A core member of the Playwright's Center, she received a 1996-97 Jerome Fellowship from the Minneapolis Playwright's Center.

She writes: A number of years ago "what's an indian woman to do?" occurred to me as a result of a daylong playwriting workshop with Spider-Woman Theatre here in Minneapolis. We riotously carried on that day, making numerous jokes about the appropriation and commericialization of native culture and spiritual beliefs by non-natives. As I went to sleep the "poem" appeared in its entirety in my brain and I jumped out of bed and wrote it down. So while I wrote the poem, I honestly don't know that it would have occurred to me without the inspiring presence of Spider-Woman. As an artist I think it is important to remember that we "feed" each other, that creative energy and thought is healing, and that humor is a tremendous tool for survival. Takonsala and mitakuye oyasin are actually Lakota words meaning "grandfather/great creator" and "all my relations"— not Ojibwe words at all (another "joke" in the whole piece).

CHILDREN'S BOOKS: *The Farmer's Market: Families Working Together* (Carolrhoda Books, 2001); *Pow Wow Summer* (CarolRhoda, 1996).

Annie Cecilia Smith is a Yakama Indian and she grew up on the Umatilla Reservation. She is a junior at Fort Lewis College, majoring in English education. She has always loved writing.

She writes of "Love is Blind": Writers know what I am talking about when I say this. Words just come to you, flowing like a river, at times.

"Frybread Queen" and "Not Indian Enough": These were essays written for a writing class I took at Blue Mountain Community College. I had the two greatest writing teachers: Bette Husted and Caroline LeGuin showed me that I could write. I didn't really follow the assignment when I wrote "Frybread Queen." But I had such a nice teacher, she let me go my own creative way. I ended up getting a good grade on that paper. "Not Indian Enough" was written as a sarcasm paper. Mrs. Husted suggested that we use dark humor. Mine turned out to be light humor. I put these two stories in the tribal newspaper in my hometown. And it felt good to see that people enjoyed what I had written. It makes me feel good that I made them laugh and lightened their day. Hopefully, someday I'll be a famous writer. Right now, I'm learning to be a teacher.

Margo Tamez is a poet and writer, born in Austin, Texas, in 1962. She is indigenous to South Texas, born of Native American (Nde-Dne) and Spanish land grant peoples who interwove their fates before and after the colonization of what is now Texas. She lives and works on a small farm that she and her family steward in southern Arizona. Born into agricultural and rural traditions of Mexican-Indian foremothers, her writing shares observations of life on the land. Her poems have appeared in *Cimarron Review* and *American Poetry Review,* among others, as well as numerous anthologies. A chapbook, *Alleys & Allies,* was published in 1991 (Saddletramp Press). She was selected as a 1998 Poetry Fellow by the Arizona Commission of the Arts. In addition to her emphasis as a poet, she contributes personal essays on a regular basis to Maricopa's small town monthly, *The Communicator.*

She explains her identity: In the 1740s Spanish land grantees originally from El Santander, Spain, colonized a part of southern Texas that other groups of Spanish colonists preferred to stay away from, due to the reputed danger of Lipan Apache people—the Tamaulipas territory (literally: Ta Ma Ho Li Pam, a Chichimeca phrase which translates as "place where the Lipan pray"). The ancestors didn't invite anyone to live in their sacred ground. And the disputes still exist within our families regarding the philosophical, spiritual, and cultural "ownership" of this territory. My paternal family members are indigenous, Coahuiltecos, relatives to those called Comanches north of the border, and Spanish and Dutch as well. I am in agreement with Ana Castillo's term: Mexic-Amerindian, which is culturally, socially, politically, and psychologically appropriate for people such as myself, similar to "Native American" in that it is a general indigenous identifier, yet it signifies particular focus to a particular group in the United States of America affected by the historical, institutional, geographical, and cultural borders of not being recognized by the Bureau of Indian Affairs. People also refer to my work as "Chicana" and "Latina," which in those contexts works for the editor's, publisher's, or audiences' purposes and needs. When one is an indigenous person of Mexican heritage in the United States there exists the ever living challenge to excavate one's consciousness of place, nativeness, community, and identity—I consider it being in a state of a persistent unveiling, a blossoming.

Laura Tohe is Diné (Navajo). She was born and raised on the Navajo reservation. She is Associate Professor in the English department at Arizona State University. Her book of poetry and stories, *No Parole Today*, received the Poetry of the Year Award by the Wordcraft Circle of Native Writers and Storytellers. She was recognized for her contributions to American Indian literature through "Those Who Speak the World into Place: An Honoring of Native Writers," made possible through Joy Harjo and the Lila Wallace–Reader's Digest Fund. She writes essays, stories, and children's plays. Her work appears in Canada and Europe. Her current work is a book of poetry and stories called *Talking Woman*. She is co-editor of *Sister Nations: Native Women Writers on Community*.

POETRY: *No Parole Today* (University of New Mexico Press, 1999).

Eulynda Toledo-Benalli is full-blooded Diné from the Diné Nation born and raised. She has three children and is married to David Benalli of Jemez Pueblo. She is working on her PH.D. in educational thought and socio-cultural studies in the College of Education at the University of New Mexico. She is an award-winning broadcast journalist focusing on features. She is co-founder of First Nations North and South, an Indigenous-led organization that seeks to reconnect our Indigenous rights by sharing our cultures, moving back and forth, north and south, before borders were set upon us. She has been a teacher with her Diné students for twenty years.

She writes of "Ashkii Nizhóní": I hope my story conveys to you the ability of Diné females to successfully live in "two worlds." Our daily lives are filled with trying to survive in today's western society yet the teachings that are embedded in our language and thought accompany us no matter where we find ourselves. Diné women hold important status in their society which plays out into the western society. Although many of us have had Diné education "schooled out" of us, we continue to have a base rooted in Changing Woman, who gave us our original clans. Thus, that very manifestation continues to remain since Creation, one of the most important aspects of Diné peoples lives.

Kim Wensaut is a member of the Forest County Wisconsin band of the Potawatomi Nation. Her poetry has appeared in *Akwe: kon, A Journal of Indigenous Issues* and *Hurricane Alice*. She works as a freelance writer for Native newspapers and is active in Potawatomi language preservation efforts.

She writes of "Alina in Kansas": This poem was written for my Potawatomi sister Alina, who moved from her woodland home to the prairies of Kansas. Her journey reminded me of the journey of our ancestors, who were forcibly removed from their homelands around Lake Michigan to the high and waterless prairies of the Midwest. This poem alludes to that journey, which is known as The Potawatomi Trail of Death. Although as a Nation we are still scattered by the storm of white "civilization," I would like to think this poem also speaks of hope, of the truth of our history and who we are as Neshnabek people, which can never be erased.

"the way around losing you": What can be said about this poem? It's just about the cure for a lonely heart: A fast motorcycle ride through the streets of San Francisco and along the hilly coast of the great wide ocean. Fun!

Karenne Wood is an enrolled member of the Monacan Indian Nation and serves on the Tribal Council. She has worked as an editorial assistant, real estate agent, domestic violence victims' advocate, and activist for the rights of women and American Indians and for environmental issues. She has studied at George Mason University and the University of Virginia and was a finalist for the Ruth Lilly Poetry Fellowship in 2000. She has contributed poems to *The American Indian Culture and Research Journal, Iris, Orion,* and *Red Ink,* and other publications. Her first book of poems won the North American Native Authors Award for Poetry.

POETRY: *Markings on Earth* (University of Arizona Press, 2001).

Evangeline Parsons Yazzie is a Navajo, originally from the community of Hardrock, Arizona, on the Navajo Reservation. She has obtained an MA in bilingual multicultural education and a PH.D. in educational leadership. She is an assistant professor of Navajo at Northern Arizona University, where she teaches mostly Navajo students wanting to learn the language of their grandparents and also native speakers whose goal it is to become literate in their own language. As a means of acknowledging and honoring her deceased parents for their gift of language, culture-knowledge, and Navajo teachings, Evangeline teaches and writes on behalf of elders and encourages others to honor their elders.

Venaya Jaye Yazzie is a member of the eastern Diné Nation of northern New Mexico, born for the Manyhogans and Bitterwater clans. She is a practicing Southwest artist, writer, and poet. She received a BA in English and communications at Fort Lewis College in Durango, Colorado. She is also an alumnus of the Institute of American Indian and Alaska Native Arts in Santa Fe, New Mexico. Her poetry has been published in *Beaver Tail Journal, The Minnesota Project-Community Connection Journal, Images Anthology, Intertribal News* and *The Denver March Powwow 2000 Magazine.*

Information on Tribes

The following is provided by the editors to give readers some idea of the historical and current locations of groups represented. Contributors have supplied their own tribal designations. Many of the web sites listed are official tribal sites; others are hosted by museums or academic organizations. The sites often provide cultural information on the roles of women within the tribe or nation. We encourage readers to visit these sites for more detailed information and for links to other sites of interest.

Abenaki

Suzanne Rancourt (Abenaki)

Abenaki bands settled widely throughout northern New England where they live today.
http://www.tolatsga.org/aben.html

Anishinaabe (also Ojibwe, Ojibway)

kateri akiwenzie-damm (Anishinaabe)
Kimberly Blaeser (Anishinaabe)
Pauline Danforth (Ojibwe)
Heid Erdrich (Ojibwe)
Lise Erdrich (Ojibway)
Louise Erdrich (Ojibwe)
Linda LeGarde Grover (Ojibwe)
Sara Littlecrow-Russell (Anishinaabe-Métis/Han)
Marcie R. Rendon (White Earth Anishinaabe)

Anishinaabe is the original name of the people commonly known as the Ojibwe, Ojibwa, Ojibway, or Chippewa. The Anishinaabe/Ojibwe people make up one of the largest tribes north of Mexico, and their

*reservations and reserves are located across the Great Lakes states
into North Dakota and southern Canada.*
http://www.tolatsga.org/ojib.html

Blackfeet

Susan Deer Cloud (Mohawk/Blackfeet)

*The Blackfeet Nation reservation is located in northern Montana
near Glacier National Park.*
www.blackfeetnation.com

Cherokee

Diane Glancy (Cherokee)
Allison Hedge Coke (Huron/Cherokee)

*The Cherokee, one of the largest tribes in North America, dominated
the southeastern states before the Civil War. In 1838 the Cherokee
were forcibly removed by the United States government to Oklahoma.
Some Cherokee, however, remained in the eastern United States,
especially in North Carolina.*
http://www.cherokee.org/Culture/History.asp

Choctaw

LeAnne Howe (Choctaw)

*The Choctaw, descendants of the mound-building people, lived in
what is now Mississippi. In the early 1830s, they were the first of the
southern tribes to be forcibly moved to Oklahoma, where their tribal
headquarters are today.*
http://www.choctawnation.com/history/history.htm

Comanche

Terry Gomez (Comanche)

The Comanche held territory from the Great Plains through Texas into Mexico. The Comanche Nation is now in Oklahoma.
http://www.tolatsga.org/ComancheOne.html

Coeur d'Alene

Teresa Iyall-Santos (Coeur d'Alene/Yakama)

The Coeur d'Alene tribe originally inhabited parts of Montana, Idaho, and Washington, where their reservation is today.
http://www.cdatribe.org/overview.html

Creek

Joy Harjo (Muscogee Creek)

The Muscogee (Creek) historically occupied the present states of Alabama, Georgia, Florida, and South Carolina. The Creek Nation is now headquartered in Oklahoma.
http://www.ocevnet.org/creek/history.html
www.colonize.com/sonarp.php3

Cree-Métis

Heather Harris (Cree-Métis)
Sara Littlecrow-Russell (Anishinaabe-Métis/Han)

Cree people are widespread in the provinces of southern Manitoba, central Saskatchewan, and Quebec, Canada.
http://www.gcc.ca/Overview/overview.htm

Métis people are a distinct population of people of Native and European ancestry who live throughout Canada and the United States.
http://www.abo-peoples.org/background/indianact.html

Dakota/Sioux

Elizabeth Cook-Lynn (Dakotah)

Nicole Ducheneaux (Sioux/Flathead)

The people of the Sioux Nation of North and South Dakota and Minnesota are also called Dakota, Lakota, or Nakota, according to their language group.

http://www.dakotacurriculum.com/Pages/Links.html

Flathead

Nicole Ducheneaux (Sioux/Flathead)

The Flathead Reservation of western Montana is home to two separate tribes: the Confederated Salish and Kootenai.

http://users.aol.com/Donh523/navapage/flathead.htm

Huron/Cherokee

Allison Hedge Coke (Huron/Cherokee)

The Huron, an eastern tribe, are part of the larger Iroquois cultural group. There are Huron populations in U. S. and Canadian communities around the Great Lakes.

http://www.tolatsga.org/hur.html

Maidu

Linda Noel (Konkow Maidu)

Maidu people, known as excellent basket makers, have lived for centuries in Northern California.

http://www.maidu.com/maidu/index.html

Mescalero Apache

Lorena Fuerta (Mescalero Apache/Yaqui)

The Mescalero Apache reservation is located in southern New Mexico.

http://www.newmexico.org/culture/res_mescalero.html

Mexican-American/Mexican-Amerindian

Margo Tamez (Mexican-Amerindian/Nde-Dne/Coahuila)

Mexican-American is a political, geographical, cultural, and historical designation that, when read literally, means Indian-American. Mexica is a Nahuatl word meaning "people." The term may also apply to Spanish-descended people who do not associate themselves with an indigenous heritage.

Mohawk

Susan Deer Cloud (Mohawk/Blackfeet)

The Mohawk are members of the Six Iroquois Nations Confederacy. Mohawk reservations and reserves are in New York and Canada
http://www.tuscaroras.com/graydeer/

Monacan

Karenne Wood (Monacan)

The Monacan Nation remains in its original homeland in Virginia.
http://members.tripod.com/monacannation/monacan.htm

Navajo

Esther Belin (Navajo)
Vee F. Browne (Navajo)
Laura Tohe (Navajo)
Eulynda Toledo-Benallie (Navajo)
Evangeline Parsons Yazzie (Navajo)
Venaya J. Yazzie (Navajo)

Navajo call themselves Diné in their own language. The homeland of the Navajo Nation is in Arizona, although there are smaller Navajo communities in other southwestern states.
http://www.americanwest.com/pages/navajo2.htm
http://www.nmcn.org/features/dinecurricula/index.html

223

Nde-Dne

Margo Tamez (Mexican-Amerindian/Nde-Dne/Coahuila)

Nde-Dne people are also known as Lipan Apache of South Texas.
http://www.indians.org/welker/lipanap.htm

Nez Perce

Ines Hernandez-Avila (Nimipu/Tejana)

*The Nez Perce Reservation in north central Idaho is home to the
people who call themselves Nimipu.*
http://www.nezperce.org/History/MainHistory.html

Oneida

Roberta Hill (Oneida)

*The Oneida Nation, originally from New York, purchased land
that eventually became their home reservation in Wisconsin near
Green Bay.*
http://www.oneidanation.org/

Potawatomi

Kim Wensaut (Potawatomi)

*Potawatomi live all over the United States with tribal lands and
communities located in Michigan, Wisconsin, and Oklahoma.*
http://www.dickshovel.com/pota.html

Pueblo

Debra Haaland (Laguna Pueblo)

*Pueblo Indians of New Mexico are settled in nineteen communities,
including Laguna.*
http://www.indianpueblo.org/
http://web.nmsu.edu/~tomlynch/swlit.laguna-history.html

Skidi/Tohono O'odham

Reva Mariah S. Gover (Skidi/Tohono O'odham)

The Skidi are one band in the Pawnee Nation. The Skidi once lived on a reservation in southern Nebraska but were later relocated to Oklahoma.
http://emuseum.mnsu.edu/cultural/northamerica/
skidi_pawnee.html

The Tohono O'odham Nation is located near Tucson, Arizona.
http://www.itcaonline.com/Tribes/tohono.htm

Yakama

Teresa Iyall-Santos (Coeur d'Alene/Yakama)
Annie Cecilia Smith (Yakama)

The tribe known as the Yakama is composed of more than a dozen bands that once had homelands throughout a huge territory in the Northwest. The Yakama Indian Reservation is in Washington.
http://www.tcfn.org/tctour/museums/Yakama.html

Yaqui

Lorena Fuerta (Mescalero Apache/Yaqui)

Yaqui people are related to the Ute-Azteca of Mexico. Yaqui homelands in the United States are in Arizona.
http://www.itcaonline.com/Tribes/pascua.htm

Notes

Introduction

1 Changing Women

Esther Belin

Kimberly Blaeser

Pauline Danforth

Allison Hedge Coke

30 **Visqueen.** Heavy sheet plastic which covers plant beds during germination and early growth.

LeAnne Howe

37 **Gullah.** A dialect spoken by African Americans in the Outer Banks region near Charleston, S.C., and many surrounding areas.

Margo Tamez

56 **Tu y Yo** *Spanish.* You and me.

2 Strong Hearts

Louise Erdrich

70 **Anishinaabeg** *Ojibwe.* Plural of Anishinaabe, meaning humans, the people's name for themselves.
71 **Gego, gego.** *Ojibwe.* Don't, don't.
72 **Manidoog** *Ojibwe.* The spirits.
    Amaniso *Ojibwe.* A portentous dream.
73 **ishkode waaboo** *Ojibwe.* Literally fire water, meaning alcoholic drinks.
74 **shkwebii** *Ojibwe.* Drunk.
    ondaas *Ojibwe.* Follow me.
76 **Gete-anishinaabeg** *Ojibwe.* The old-time people, the ancient Anishinaabeg.
77 **n'dede** *Ojibwe.* My daddy.

Linda LeGarde Grover

83 **Indizhinikaaz Kwiiwizens** *Ojibwe.* My name is Kwiiwizens (Young Boy).
    gaye indizhinikaaz Chi-Ko-ko-koho *Ojibwe.* And I am called Chi-Ko-ko-koho.
    Ni maajaa. Mi-iw *Ojibwe.* I leave. That is all.

Debra Haaland

85 **piki** *Keres.* A flat bread made from blue, red, or yellow corn batter and cooked on a large flat granite stone, which has been heated by fire.
86 **Jemez.** One of the Northern Pueblos of New Mexico, located approximately 50 miles northwest of Albuquerque.
    Laguna. A Western Pueblo of New Mexico, consisting of six villages and located 40 miles west of Albuquerque.

87   **Hopi.** A Pueblo located in eastern Arizona.

88   **chongo** *Keres.* Term for a hairstyle in which the long hair is gathered behind the neck, folded, and secured with either string, yarn, or a piece of woven wool cloth.

Inés Hernández-Avila

96   **Indi'n.** Slang for Indian.

97   **walah'tsa** *Nez Perce.* Seven Drum tradition.
      Seven Drums. The Seven Drum tradition is "old way" Nez Perce, according to my family, and it is called such because there are seven drummers/singers who officiate on special occasions or lead ceremonies.

Laura Tohe

100   **Dinétah** *Diné/Navajo.* Navajo homeland.
      Ałkidą́ą' adajiní nít'ę́ę̀ *Diné/Navajo.* They say a long time ago.
      Sis Naajiní *Diné/Navajo.* White Shell Mountain, also known as Blanca Peak.
      Tsoodził *Diné/Navajo.* Turquoise Mountain, also known as Mount Taylor.
      Dook'o'oosłííd *Diné/Navajo.* Abalone Shell Mountain, also known as San Francisco Mountain.
      Dibé Nítsaa *Diné/Navajo.* Obsidian Mountain, also known as La Plata Mountain.

102   **Bi'éé' Lichii'í** *Diné/Navajo.* Red Shirt, also known as Kit Carson.

103   **Hweełdi** *Diné/Navajo.* Place of extreme hardship.

3   New Age Pocahontas

Terry Gomez

124   **Kiowa.** Plains tribe now in Oklahoma.
      Kah-koo *Comanche.* Grandmother on the mother's side.

Linda LeGarde Grover

133   **Ikwe Ishpiming** *Ojibwe.* Woman Heaven or Woman's Heaven.
      asi anang *Ojibwe.* Shining star.
      ambe *Ojibwe.* Come here.
      ambe omaa, bimosen, bimosen *Ojibwe.* Come here, walk, walk.
      wewiib *Ojibwe.* Hurry.

134   **oshki-traditional** *Ojibwe and English.* New or neo traditional.

Teresa Iyall-Santos

136 **Yay-Yay** *Salish.* Maternal Grandmother.
Ohh-Neh! *Salish.* Look at this, it is worthy!

Sara Littlecrow-Russell

137 **Rez.** Short for reservation, the Native American lands reserved by treaty.

Marcie Rendon

138 **takonsala** [*sic:* see Contributors] *Dakota.* Grandfather.
mitakuye oyasin *Dakota.* All My Relations.
jeebik *Ojibwe.* Possibly slang for "putting magic on" or "putting medicine on."

Annie Cecilia Smith

143 **rez car.** Term in common use among tribes, usually an older model car with rust, dents, etc.
enit. Tag word in common use among tribes, usually comes at the end of a sentence to ask agreement.

4 In the Arms of the Skies

Esther Belin

156 **doulas** *English/Spanish.* Midwives.

Vee F. Browne

159 **Yidlohgo t'óó shi? nizhóní yee'** *Diné/Navajo.* When you smile, it is beautiful for me.

Diane Glancy

160 **Kicking Bear.** Speech quoted in *Indian Oratory,* compiled by W. C. Vanderwerth (Norman: University of Oklahoma Press, 1989).

Sara Littlecrow-Russell

184 **intertribal.** Pow-wow term in common use among tribes: a social dance for everyone.

Eulynda Toledo-Benalli

189 **Ashkii Nizhóní** *Diné/Navajo.* Handsome boy.
Shimá sání *Diné/Navajo.* My grandmother (maternal).
Bízhí' *Diné/Navajo.* Paternal aunt.
Shizhé'é yázhí *Diné/Navajo.* Paternal uncle.

190 **Nakaiłbáhí** *Diné/Navajo*. Mexican.

Nálí *Diné/Navajo*. Can mean either paternal grandmother or paternal grandfather.

Enemy Way ceremony. Navajo ceremony for protection and healing.

193 **Shitsilí daats'í' nílí, shinaí dats'í** *Diné/Navajo*. You might be my younger brother, you might be my older brother.

Shizhé'í *Diné/Navajo*. My father.

194 **Hágoónee', ya** *Diné/Navajo*. Goodbye, okay.

Sister Nations was designed and set in type by Cathy Spengler, Minneapolis. The typeface is Figural, designed by Oldrich Menhart in 1940. This book was printed by Maple Press, York, Pennsylvania.